DECADES

T0246514

Rick Wakeman

in the 1970s

Geoffrey Feakes

sonicbondpublishing.com

Sonicbond Publishing Limited
www.sonicbondpublishing.co.uk
Email: info@sonicbondpublishing.co.uk

First Published in the United Kingdom 2023
First Published in the United States 2023

British Library Cataloguing in Publication Data:
A Catalogue record for this book is available from the British Library

Copyright Geoffrey Feakes 2023

ISBN 978-1-78952-264-8

Typeset in ITC Garamond Std & ITC Avant Garde Gothic Pro
Printed and bound in England
Graphic design and typesetting: Full Moon Media

DECADES

Rick Wakeman

in the 1970s

Geoffrey Feakes

sonicbondpublishing.com

Follow us on social media:
Twitter: https://twitter.com/SonicbondP
Instagram: https://www.instagram.com/sonicbondpublishing_/
Facebook: https://www.facebook.com/SonicbondPublishing/

Linktree QR code:

DECADES | Rick Wakeman in the 1970s

Contents

Introduction

For as long as I can remember I always wanted to be a musician of one
sort or another.
Rick Wakeman – *Say Yes!* autobiography published in 1995.

Mention the name Rick Wakeman in mixed company and you will
no doubt elicit a mixed response. To some, he is a television and
radio personality renowned for his cringe-worthy jokes and grumpy
demeanour. To others, including your author and hopefully you,
dear reader, he is one of the most talented, technically accomplished
musicians and composers to have graced the world of popular music
over the past five decades.

When he came to prominence in the early 1970s, Rick was that rare
find, a genuine progressive rock superstar who consistently topped
reader's polls in the music magazines. To date, taking into account
compilations, studio and live recordings, he has a staggering 130
albums or more to his credit. Understandably, given such a vast body of
work, quality control has been variable at times, although the majority
of his output is worthy of investigation. This book focuses on Rick's
career in the 1970s when, in his twenties, he was at the peak of his
creative powers. In addition to his solo activities – which included
eight albums – he was pivotal in shaping the sound of progressive rock
pioneers Yes and played no small part in their international success as
a 1970s supergroup. Before that, Rick was a prolific session musician,
contributing to songs by David Bowie, Elton John and Cat Stevens,
amongst many others and he was also a member of the highly regarded
folk rock band Strawbs. But let's wind the clock back some twenty-plus
years earlier.

Richard Christopher Wakeman was born in Perivale, West London, on
18 May 1949. An only child, he lived with his parents in the suburb of
Northolt, just ten miles from central London and the heart of the British
entertainment industry. Although the second world war had ended
four years earlier, rationing in the UK was still part of everyday life.
Despite the austerity of the times, the Wakeman household was a stable,
comfortable environment and like many respectable suburbanites, they
were regular church goers. Young Richard was in awe of the deep,
reverberating sound of the pipe organ and 'The day thou gavest, Lord, is
ended' was one of his mother Mildred's favourite hymns.

Rick's piano talents were apparent from an early age and his father, Cyril Frank Wakeman, enrolled him in private lessons at the age of six. His teacher, Dorothy Symes, taught him how to interpret the classical composers and she would be his mentor for the next 15 years. In the *Caped Crusader* biography Rick confirmed: 'My piano playing is very Mozart, but I think I've basically been influenced by everybody's music I've played, which is every classical composer in the book'. He proved to be a child prodigy and aged just nine, he passed with distinction The Royal School of Music grade one piano exam in March 1959. When he entered and won his first competition – the Southall Music Festival – at the age of ten, it would be the first of many such triumphs over the ensuing years.

Rick attended Drayton Manor Grammar School in Hanwell, west London and during his later years there, he moonlighted in the evenings as a pianist in the local pubs and clubs. Because of his lofty stature, he could pass himself off as an older person. In tandem with his music, he also had a passion for sports, especially football, and at weekends he could often be found on the terraces supporting his favourite team, Brentford Football Club.

In 1963, Rick co-founded a school traditional jazz band – the short-lived Brother Wakeman and the Clergymen – even though he never really developed a passion for jazz, traditional or modern. A stint with another local group – the Atlantic Blues – followed, in which Rick was now playing the electric organ – a cut-price model purchased from Woolworths department store. He left the group to join The Conchord Quartet and the money from a twice-weekly booking allowed Rick to invest in his first proper instrument, a £40 Hohner Pianet electric piano. Soon after, the hastily assembled Curdled Milk – a pun on the band name Cream – made their one and only appearance at the school's end-of-year sixth-form dance.

Rick had his sights set on becoming a concert pianist and after working hard to achieve the required school grades and passing the entrance exams, he entered London's esteemed Royal College of Music. He didn't get on with the piano teacher, however, who was also offended by the length of his hair, and he maintained his private studies with Mrs Symes. It was a requirement of the college to be proficient on two instruments, but Rick's clarinet skills were lacking compared with his prestigious piano talents.

At the age of 17, Rick became the youngest member of the Ronnie Smith show band, his first professional group. They performed at the

Top Rank dance halls that were popular in the UK in the 1960s. He and the singer Ashley Holt became firm friends in this environment and would team up again in 1973. It was here that Rick developed his showmanship tendencies, rocking the Hammond organ back and forth to agitate the reverb unit and running a paint roller over the keyboard, much to Ronnie Smith's exasperation. After Smith gave him his marching orders, Rick joined the Tony Dee Showband managed by Dave Simms, who also ran the Musical Bargain Centre in South Ealing, London, a popular hangout for local musicians.

In early 1968, Rick was in his second term at the Royal College of Music and was finding it hard to balance his daytime academic duties with his nocturnal activities as a jobbing musician. At the Bargain Centre, he met bass player Chas Cronk and it was his recommendation that secured Rick's first recording session. It was at Olympic Studios in London for soul singer Jimmy Thomas, a one-time member of Ike and Tina Turner's backing band. The song was 'The Running Kind' and the producer Denny Cordell had an impressive portfolio, including The Moody Blues' debut album. Rick played the studio's Hammond organ and wrote the brass arrangements, and it was during the session that he met producer Tony Visconti who would figure regularly in Rick's recording career over the coming years. As his reputation grew, lucrative session work came flooding in and Rick was soon skipping lectures at the Royal College of Music. Eventually, he made the life-changing decision to abandon his studies and pursue a full-time career as a rock musician.

Rick re-joined Ronnie Smith's band towards Christmas 1968, who by now had a residency at the Top Rank in Reading, 50 miles west of London. It was here that Rick met his future wife, Rosalind Woolford, who worked behind the bar. His four nights each week in Reading were supplemented with three nights of solo pub gigs along with the daytime sessions. The exhaustive work ethic enabled Rick to purchase his first Hammond organ, an L100. In 1969, he was introduced to David Bowie and played the legendary Mellotron arrangement on the song 'Space Oddity' and was rewarded with a cheque for £9 from producer Gus Dudgeon. Tony Visconti, who declined to produce 'Space Oddity', recommended Rick for the session. In the book *David Bowie: A Life* by Dylan Jones, Rick explained:

I did a session for Tony Visconti in 1968 for a band called Junior's Eyes. There was a Mellotron in the studio, and they were very new at the time, so I played around with it for a couple of hours. I knew about the problems they had keeping them in tune, but after a while, I found a way you could cheat to keep it in tune; it was a mixture of doing arpeggios with your fingers, making sure there's always two notes being held down at the same time, and playing with a pitch control. Then when David started recording 'Space Oddity', he wanted a Mellotron mixed in with everything else, but couldn't keep the thing in tune. That's when Tony Visconti called me.

After once again being fired from Ronnie Smith's band, Rick joined the group Spinning Wheel in response to an ad in the music weekly *Melody Maker*. They played seven nights a week at the Greyhound pub in Ilford with a repertoire that included the popular songs of the day. The pay was generous, £40 a week, which was more than double the average UK wage at the time. This, coupled with his session work, meant that life for the blonde keyboardist was looking up.

1970 - A Man for All Seasons

Rick was about to generate a seismic shift in the music world, and
more especially that of Strawbs.
Dave Cousins, from his autobiography *Exorcising Ghosts,* published
in 2014.

As the 1970s dawned, Rick Wakeman, aged just 20, already had hundreds
of recordings as a session musician under his belt. 'Fixer' David Katz,
who sourced musicians for record producers, was instrumental in
ensuring Rick received regular work, which included performing on
TV themes for popular series like *The Avengers* and *Jason King.* Some
of the pop and novelty acts he recorded for including White Plains,
Edison Lighthouse, Brotherhood of Man, The Fortunes, Cilla Black and
Mary Hopkin enjoyed hit singles, but his contributions went uncredited.
Although he was usually hired for his playing and arranging skills, he
wrote and performed the jaunty theme tune for the BBC TV series *Ask
Aspel*, a popular family entertainment programme during the 1970s.
     Despite his unorthodox appearance and casual demeanour, Rick
earned the respect and admiration of the producers and musicians he
worked with. He was nicknamed 'One-take Wakeman' because of his
uncanny ability to nail his parts first time and he could often be found in
the pub across the road while the others were still in the studio working
on theirs. In between sessions, he was still appearing nightly on stage,
but as the groups he'd performed with thus far never ventured beyond
the club circuit, his public profile as a musician – let alone a rock star –
was minimal. This was about to change, however.
     Although he was earning good money with Spinning Wheel, Rick
was getting tired of playing every night to the same pub audiences and
yearned to be part of a proper touring band. He was briefly a member
of Warhorse, fronted by Ashley Holt, who he had befriended back in the
days of the Ronnie Smith band, but this came to nought. Given that the
following year, Rick revealed to *Melody Maker* journalist Mark Plumber 'I
hate folk music', his next move, in hindsight, seems like an unusual one.
     Strawbs, unlike many of their folk-rock contemporaries, performed
original songs, many penned by band leader and frontman Dave
Cousins. They had evolved from the Strawberry Hill Boys, a bluegrass
combo who were part of the London folk scene in the 1960s. Strawbs
were handled by E.G. management and had the distinction of being the

first UK act signed by American label A&M Records. Like Ian Anderson of Jethro Tull, Cousins has a very distinctive voice that one immediately associates with British folk and like Rick, he was a session musician in the late 1960s working through David Katz. When interviewed by *Melody Maker* in 1970, Cousins acknowledged:

> I suppose my songs are old-fashioned, out of date, but then again, they aren't. I don't deliberately set out to write a song to sound as though it were from some different age, it just comes out that way. … We'll play every instrument we can. One minute we've got dulcimer and piano and tablas, and the next something completely different.

In his biography *The Caped Crusader,* published in 1978, Rick told author Dan Wooding: '…Dave Cousins is probably the best lyricist this century musically. I thought he wrote incredibly nice melodies – but I don't think the way they were treated was very good'.

Rick's gradual induction into the ranks of Strawbs included a guest appearance on their second album *Dragonfly.* He plays piano on the ten-minute-plus 'The Vision of The Lady of the Lake' that dominates side two of the original vinyl LP. Strawbs utilised an unusual combination of instruments to ensure a unique sound that set them apart from the folk mainstream. The line-up for *Dragonfly* is Dave Cousins on vocals, acoustic guitar, dulcimer, percussion, Tony Hooper on vocals, acoustic and electric guitars, percussion, Claire Deniz on cello and Ron Chesterman on double bass. In addition to Rick, guests Paul Brett from Velvet Opera and Danish jazz man Bjarne Rostvold play lead guitar and drums respectively on 'The Vision of The Lady of the Lake'.

The backing track was recorded in the latter part of 1969 at Ivar Rosenberg Lydteknik in Copenhagen, but they ran out of studio time, so it was completed at Morgan Studios in London. Producer Tony Visconti booked Rick to play piano, but they encountered a major problem. In his autobiography *Exorcising Ghosts*, Dave Cousins takes up the story:

> The eight-track machine was running at a slightly different speed to the one in Denmark. There was no vari-speed facility to correct it, so Rick's piano sounded completely out of tune. Tony Visconti came up with the ingenious solution of playing the piano back through a Leslie speaker so that no one noticed that it was out of tune. Instead, it had a strange ethereal, psychedelic sound that suited the track anyway.

'The Vision of The Lady of the Lake' begins as an acoustic ballad with bowed double bass, dual acoustic guitars, and mournful cello. Thanks to Visconti's unusual treatment, Rick's piano is virtually unrecognisable. Cousins' poetic lyrics tell the tale of a boatman who encounters a mysterious maiden who rises from the lake. She gives him a sword and he fights a succession of creatures, including an eagle, a snake, and a wolf, before succumbing to a watery grave. As Cousins' lead vocal becomes more impassioned, Rostvold's busy drum pattern enters at the five-minute mark, joined by Brett's distorted lead guitar.

Although it did not chart, when *Dragonfly* – which Cousins later described as 'acid folk' – was released in the UK on 16 February 1970, it did respectable business, shifting 19,000 units. Despite being an experienced session musician, it was the first time Rick's name appeared on a record sleeve and he was so grateful he wrote to Cousins thanking him, although they had first met in January 1969 when Tony Visconti brought Rick along to a BBC Radio One session for John Peel's *Top Gear* show to promote Strawbs' forthcoming eponymous debut album. Visconti was enamoured by Rick's talent and used him at every opportunity. He also admired Rick's social skills, as he confirmed in his 2007 autobiography: 'I always liked Rick; he had a refreshing 'just-one-of-the-lads' personality and could drink most of us under the table at the pub'. Rick plays organ on the three songs recorded for the Peel session, which feature as bonus tracks on the 2008 reissue of *Strawbs*. Cousins confirmed:

> We played our epic, 'The Battle', the six-minute-long closing track on Strawbs, and I knew we had recorded something special. After the session, we adjourned to the nearest pub for a celebratory drink – Rick was wide-eyed, enthusiastic, enjoyed several pints and was one of the lads, as we say. I made a note to stay in touch with him.

In March 1970, shortly after the release of *Dragonfly*, Cousins contacted Rick and they arranged to meet in the Greenford Hotel pub – now a McDonalds – on the Uxbridge Road in Southall, West London. Cousins remembers the occasion well:

> Rick turned up with Ros, who he introduced as his fiancée. We exchanged pleasantries over a couple of pints, and then I asked him if he fancied joining Strawbs. Rick's hand, holding his pint, was shaking like

a leaf as he accepted my generous offer of £12 ($20) a week. I told him that I wanted his first gigs with Strawbs to be something memorable.

In *The Caped Crusader* biography, Rick recalls that Cousins' offer was £25 a week. Otherwise, the details of the meeting remain the same. When Cousins explained that the band were going to Paris the following month, Rick initially declined because he and Ros were getting married on 28 March. They couldn't afford a honeymoon, however, so Cousins suggested a compromise whereby Ros accompanied Rick to Paris.

Rick's debut gig on 5 April with Strawbs was billed as the 'Open Circus' and was held in a big top on the Champ du Mars by the Eiffel Tower. The other bands on the bill included East of Eden and Pete Brown's Piblokto. They each had to accompany the circus acts and Strawbs were allocated the child jugglers, a lion wrestler, and a high-wire act. Without a drummer in the band, Rick had to time his solo during 'Where Is This Dream of Your Youth' – from the debut *Strawbs* album – to reach a crescendo when the wire walker did a forward roll. On the second day, during Rick's solo, the audience began to cheer when none other than Salvador Dali walked onto the stage. Rick was less than impressed, however and not knowing who Dali was, and he suggested in colourful language that the famous painter be escorted from the stage.

Rick's first UK gig with Strawbs was also his first television appearance for the show *Songs from the Two Brewers*. It was filmed in the upstairs room of a pub in Manchester, just around the corner from the Granada TV studio. Legendary folk singer Ralph McTell was present and was stunned by Rick's playing when he launched into his solo on upright piano during the folky 'Till the Sun Comes Shining Through' from *Dragonfly*. Although Rick recalls audience figures being low on those early shows, a critic for *Melody Maker* praised his performance at Birmingham Town Hall:

> I was particularly impressed by Rick Wakeman's solo contribution at the piano, used three days previously by Count Basie. Mainly a straight piano number, this unnamed composition ranged through Grieg-ish passages and a stomping blues.

The number in question would later be titled 'Temperament of Mind' and would become Rick's solo showpiece during his tenure with Strawbs.

Although he was now a full-time Strawb, the session work continued at a hectic pace and along with the pop acts, such was his versatility that Rick also recorded for the folk fraternity. This included the album *Scenery* by obscure trio Paper Bubble, produced by Dave Cousins and Tony Hooper and he plays organ and piano on *Seasons*, the second album by Magna Carta, who were in a more progressive folk vein. He also recorded for American folk singer and guitarist Shawn Phillips, a fellow A&M label artist who went down a storm at the 1970 Isle of Wight Festival. Along with a host of prog rock's finest, including Jon Anderson, Peter Gabriel, Peter Hammill, Phil Collins and Robert Fripp, Rick also contributed to the eponymous debut album by Colin Scot, which was released the following year.

One of the oddest recordings he was involved with is the collectable single 'Oh Baby' b/w 'Universal Love' by Dib Cochran & The Earwigs, which was released in August 1970. It features Tony Visconti – alias Dib Cochran – on bass and vocals, Marc Bolan – of T. Rex fame – on guitar and Rick on piano. It's tongue-in-cheek and very different to the *Changes* album by classical guitar maestro John Williams that Rick was particularly proud to be involved with. Released in 1971, it features the cream of UK session musicians and Rick and several others later joined Williams at London's Royal Festival Hall for a charity show in aid of War on Want.

Strawbs – Just a Collection of Antiques and Curios

Personnel:
Dave Cousins: vocals, acoustic guitar, electric guitar, dulcimer
Tony Hooper: vocals, acoustic guitar, tambourine
Rick Wakeman: piano, organ, harpsichord, celeste
Richard Hudson: vocals, drums, congas, percussion, sitar
John Ford: vocals, bass guitar
Recorded live at the Queen Elizabeth Hall, London
Produced by Tony Visconti
Recording date: 11 July 1970
Release date: October 1970
Record label: A&M
Highest chart places: UK: 27, USA: Did not chart
Running time: 40:44
All tracks written by Dave Cousins, except as noted otherwise
Side one: 1. Martin Luther King's Dream (2:53), 2. The Antique Suite: The

Reaper, We Must Cross the River, Antiques and Curios, Hey It's Been a Long Time (12:12), 3. Temperament of Mind (4:50) (Rick Wakeman). Side two: 1. Fingertips (6:14), 2. Song of a Sad Little Girl (5:28), 3. Where Is This Dream of Your Youth (9:07)

Following the recording of *Dragonfly*, cellist Claire Deniz and double bassist Ron Chesterman decided that life on the road in a rock band was not for them and left Strawbs. Chesterman's replacement Lindsay Cooper had also come and gone. For Cousins, it was an opportunity to beef up the band's rhythm section with the acquisition of a drummer and electric bass player. Being versatile musicians and singer-songwriters, Richard Hudson and John Ford fitted the bill perfectly and came to Strawbs via psychedelic rockers Elmer Gantry's Velvet Opera. The pair would play a significant part in steering the band even further from their folk roots.

Strawbs first rehearsal as a five-piece was in May 1970 in the front room of Cousins' home in Hounslow, West London. He wrote 'Song of a Sad Little Girl' for his daughter Joelle in one of his favoured D modal tunings where the six open strings of the guitar, lowest to highest, are tuned to the notes D, A, D, G, A, D. Rick was initially puzzled by the opening chords, but when he started rippling single notes over the guitar part, it was the beginning of what Cousins described as 'the Strawbs sound'. The four-part 'The Antique Suite' was also rehearsed, as was 'Where Is This Dream of Your Youth', a showcase for Rick. The set was initially tested at the Hounslow Arts Lab and although the audience reaction was encouraging, the club was subsequently closed by the police due to the excessive noise.

E.G., who also had King Crimson and Emerson, Lake & Palmer on their books, let Strawbs go and their new management Arnakata booked them on a prestigious three-week nationwide tour of major halls supporting Roy Harper. Rick was asserting himself from a visual perspective, climbing on top of his Hammond L100 while still playing it, à la Keith Emerson. With his brightly coloured bell bottoms and tee shirts, imposing height, and long blonde hair, he certainly stood out.

One particular event on the 23 May played an important part in shaping Rick's future. A power cut at Sheffield University – or Sheffield City Hall, depending upon which source you trust – interrupted the set and he responded with an impromptu piano solo. Enthusiastically received, it became a permanent fixture in the band's setlist during Rick's tenure. A later performance on the Roy Harper tour featuring

Rick's solo was recorded and released as the *Recollection* live album in 2006. It features several songs not included in the *Just a Collection of Antiques and Curios* live set recorded just a few weeks later.

Exactly two months after the first rehearsal, the five-piece Strawbs played their first ever headline gig on Saturday, 11 July. The venue was the Queen Elizabeth Hall on London's South Bank, which normally hosted classical concerts. The performance, which includes mostly previously unreleased material, was recorded for posterity using a mobile unit outside the venue. The capacity audience witnessed Rick's expanded keyboard rig, which included organ, piano, harpsichord and celeste and his grand piano solo 'Temperament of Mind' received a standing ovation. The review in *The Guardian* newspaper the following day by Robin Denselow summed up the critic's reaction to Rick's performance:

The one really startling new talent that does emerge from the Strawbs is Rick Wakeman. He was allowed one solo spot, which he devoted to a dazzling and very funny musical spoof.

Melody Maker was equally enthusiastic:

Watch out for Rick Wakeman. He has a near mastery of the keyboard. The capacity audience sat motionless as he wrestled with the organ, flooding the hall with a torrent of sound. When he turned his attention to piano, it was equally effective.

Three weeks later, on 31 July, Strawbs played London's Lyceum Theatre where *Melody Maker* reported that Keith Emerson had booked a box to check out this young rival. In his autobiography *Pictures of an Exhibitionist*, Emerson claimed he missed Rick's performance, but the following week at the same venue, the two legendary keyboardists met for the first time. Emerson admitted: 'Maybe there were a few journalistic errors, but I remained a little suspicious of Rick for some time. He was, after all, competition'.

On Saturday, 8 August, Strawbs were one of many acts at the four-day National Jazz and Blues Festival, which also included Black Sabbath, Deep Purple and Yes. Rick was attracting so much attention that on 22 August, he was pictured on the front cover of *Melody Maker* with the headline 'Tomorrow's superstar?'

Just a Collection of Antiques and Curios was the first Strawbs album
to enter the UK chart and although it remained for just two weeks,
peaking at number 27 on 21 November, it sold a more than respectable
32,000 copies. It was also their first release in America, a bold move
considering it was a live recording. The critics that had been bowled
over by the concert were equally enthusiastic over the album. The
cover photograph features a collection of personal items from the band
members, including Rick's clarinet, the instrument he struggled to
master at the Royal College of Music. He was unhappy with his black
and white headshot on the back of the original pressing, so it was
replaced with a more congenial image of the band enjoying a pint in the
London Apprentice pub in Isleworth.

The album opens in fine style with 'Martin Luther King's Dream',
Cousins' acoustic lament to the civil rights leader who was shot dead
in 1968. Visconti's production is crystal clear, capturing Cousins'
impassioned vocals echoing around the auditorium. Tony Hooper,
Richard Hudson, and John Ford provide sublime vocal support,
enhancing the song's folk lilt while Rick pitches in with a tasteful, if a
tad subdued, organ break. Clearly, he was just warming up.

The subject of 'The Antique Suite' is an elderly man nearing the end
of his life, surrounded by possessions that bring back memories of the
past. It was inspired by Cousins' visit to the house of a retired doctor
in Southall, Middlesex. Despite Hudson's prominent conga drums, the
opening section 'The Reaper' has a Renaissance ambience thanks to
Rick's inspired harpsichord playing. A wordless choral chant leads into
the second part, 'We Must Cross the River' featuring dulcimer and sweet
harmonies. It has an early Simon & Garfunkel vibe, lifted by a memorable
choral hook. Cousins sings the measured 'Antiques and Curios' before
close harmonies signal the final part 'Hey It's Been a Long Time'. It floats
on a cushion of acoustic guitars, celeste and Ford's articulate bass lines as
the elderly gentleman recalls the true love he was separated from during
the war. Tony Hooper leads the band for the singalong chorus with
honky tonk piano to bring the piece to a rousing close.

Side one of the original vinyl LP concludes with Rick's solo showcase,
'Temperament of Mind'. A combination of classical themes and comedy,
the piece was so called because when performed live, Rick would often
vary the arrangement depending upon his mood and the reaction of the
audience. It begins with elaborate piano textures before hitting its up-
tempo stride and taking a diversion into swing jazz territory. A snippet

of Bach's 'Air on a G-string' develops into a homage to silent movie themes, including the iconic 'The Big Chase' which dates back to 1914. It's a stunning performance, rounded off with a flurry of cascading notes, earning the most rapturous applause of the evening.

Opening side two, 'Fingertips' is replete with sexually charged lyrics like 'Her legs the spreading branches of the tree of life'. During the lengthy instrumental outro, Hudson's George Harrison-inspired sitar brings a touch of the psychedelic to the table and, as the chocolate advert used to say, it's 'full of Eastern promise'. 'Song of a Sad Little Girl' is a delightful ballad with Rick's one-minute-twenty-seconds piano intro rippling with taste and restraint. The intro was edited for the original LP but thankfully was reinstated in its entirety for the CD reissue. In the song, Cousins' daughter is suffering from a bout of night-time illness before waking with the morning light to the sound of lush Strawbs harmonies.

The concluding 'Where Is This Dream of Your Youth' features Cousins' funky electric guitar riff, a far cry from the band's acoustic roots. The song is dominated by Rick's electrifying six-and-a-half minute semi-improvised Hammond solo. Backed by a shuffle rhythm in the style of Santana, he lays down volleys of fuzzed organ, utilising distortion and reverb delivered with wild abandon, echoing Keith Emerson's stage theatrics.

The concert and album not only signpost Rick's future as a technically versatile musician, but they also demonstrate his flair for showmanship which would peak in the mid-1970s. The solo during the extended 'Where Is This Dream of Your Youth' would also prove to be the longest, and arguably most indulgent, of his career. Interviewed by Penny Valentine in 1970 for the recently launched *Sounds* music weekly, Rick said: 'I have always tried to play something nobody else can play, I think I've based all my organ work on that kind of attitude'.

Just a Collection of Antiques and Curios was in good company in 1970. Spearheading the burgeoning progressive rock scene, Yes and Genesis released their second albums and King Crimson their third, while Emerson, Lake & Palmer made their impressive debut. The Moody Blues topped the UK chart with *A Question of Balance* as did Pink Floyd's *Atom Heart Mother* and *Led Zeppelin III*, both released the same month as the Strawbs' album. Competition on the folk rock front came from Fairport Convention, Roy Harper and Pentangle, along with debut albums from Steeleye Span and Lindisfarne. On the other side of the Atlantic, American folk rock was personified by *Déjà Vu* by Crosby, Stills, Nash & Young, *After the Gold Rush* by Neil Young and *Self*

Portrait by Bob Dylan. None however could compete with the success of Simon & Garfunkel's *Bridge Over Troubled Water,* which swept the board in both the album and singles charts in 1970.

The 1987 CD reissue of *Just a Collection of Antiques and Curios* includes live versions of 'The Vision of the Lady of the Lake' and 'We'll Meet Again Sometime'. They were recorded at the same Queen Elizabeth Hall concert but omitted from the original release due the time constraints of vinyl. Also included on the reissue is the Bee Gees-like 'Forever' which was released as a single in 1970. A big ballad pastiche replete with strings, it's a million miles from the familiar Strawbs sound.

Life on the road continued at a hectic pace for the band and on one occasion, a gig at London's Regents Park College was followed by a 200-mile drive for a late-night performance at Leeds University Fresher Ball. To add insult to injury, they were refused entry into their hotel because they hadn't checked in the evening before and had to drive straight back to London.

It was around this time that Rick bought a Hammond C3 organ, and the band swapped their Transit van for a Mercedes truck to transport their gear along with the services of a two-man road crew. On 9 December, Strawbs supported Yes at Hull City Hall and Cousins remembers Jon Anderson and company watching Rick intently from the side of the stage. Rick was similarly impressed by Yes' performance, noting their unique presentation and sound that set them apart from the more conventional rock bands of the day.

A busy year for Strawbs ended on a high with a headlining performance at London's prestigious Royal Albert Hall in aid of the Conservation Society. The support act was Scottish folk singer Al Stewart whose fourth album, *Orange* released in January 1972, would include piano and organ contributions from Rick.

By the close of 1970, Rick had established himself as a fully integrated member of Strawbs, both musically and socially. His infectious sense of humour bubbled over on and off stage and despite his slim frame, he had an insatiable appetite, fuelled by spicy curries washed down with copious amounts of beer. Although he was not a user of recreational drugs, he remained a compulsive cigarette smoker until 1978. He also enjoyed the simple pleasures of life, like watching Brentford FC play on Saturday afternoons and spending Sunday lunchtimes in the pub playing darts. A favourite weekend haunt was the White Bear in Hounslow, where Dave Cousins had started a folk club in the 1960s. According to Cousins, when Rick wasn't tickling the ivories, he was equally nimble when manipulating the flippers on a pinball machine.

1971 - Onwards and Upwards

It was a great period. A time of tour, record, and tour some more…
it was another level…everybody was playing in a way they'd never
played before.
Rick in *Prog* magazine in 2021.

Pick any year from the 1970s and it would be a significant one for
Rick. Even though he had yet to kick start his solo career, 1971 would
prove to be particularly eventful. He began the year as a member of one
band and finished it as a member of another. In between, he recorded
milestone albums with both bands, crossed the Atlantic for the first time
and participated in his most acclaimed session work.

At the beginning of 1971, Cousins and the other Strawbs members
noticed a marked change in their usually easy-going keyboard player.
He became tense and difficult, and the gregarious lifestyle coupled with
the unremitting work rate and unsociable hours, was beginning to affect
his health. Nonetheless, duty called and in January, Strawbs entered the
studio to begin work on Rick's first and last, full-length studio album
with the band.

Strawbs - From the Witchwood
Personnel:
Dave Cousins: lead vocals, backing vocals, acoustic guitar, electric guitar,
dulcimer, banjo, recorder
Tony Hooper: lead vocals, backing vocals, acoustic guitar, autoharp,
tambourine
Rick Wakeman: piano, organ, celeste, Mellotron, Moog synthesizer,
clavinet, harpsichord
Richard Hudson: lead vocals, backing vocals, drums, sitar
John Ford: lead vocals, backing vocals, bass guitar
Additional personnel:
The Choir and Congregation of Air Strawb: choir on 'A Glimpse of Heaven'
Produced at Air Studios, London by Tony Visconti
Recording date: February – March 1971
Release date: July 1971
Record label: A&M
Highest chart places: UK: 39, USA: Did not chart
Running time: 38:11

All tracks written by Dave Cousins, except as noted otherwise
Side one: 1. A Glimpse of Heaven (3:50), 2. Witchwood (3:20), 3. Thirty Days
(2:50) (John Ford), 4. Flight (4:25) (Richard Hudson), 5. The Hangman and
the Papist (4:10). Side two: 1. Sheep (4:14), 2. Canon Dale (3:46) (Hudson),
3. The Shepherd's Song (4:34), 4. In Amongst the Roses (3:48), 5. I'll Carry on
Beside You (3:09)

Strawbs fourth album *From the Witchwood,* was recorded in the recently
opened Air Studios in the West End of London under the watchful
eye of producer Tony Visconti. Rick assembled a formidable array of
keyboards for the recording, a pointer to the set-up he would play with
Yes and his solo projects over the coming years. Dave Cousins' imposed
compositional domination is balanced by songs from John Ford and
Richard Hudson, although conspicuously, there are no contributions
from previous song writing collaborator Tony Hooper or Rick.

The opening song 'A Glimpse of Heaven' was also the first to be
recorded, featuring a blistering organ solo around the halfway mark.
'The Hangman and the Papist' was another early recording and
according to Cousins, was captured in one take. The studio boasted a
Mellotron and a modular Moog synthesiser and both were utilised on
album highlight 'The Shepherd's Song'. Rick had previously played
Mellotron on the album *Battersea Power Station* by proto-proggers
Junior's Eyes as well as David Bowie's 'Space Oddity' and although
it was a notoriously temperamental instrument, he had devised a
technique of keeping it in tune. The huge Moog was a more daunting
proposition, but with Visconti's assistance and an hour or so of
tinkering, he was able to simulate the tone of a piccolo trumpet to
complement the Mellotron strings.

The recording sessions were interrupted by a concert at the Paradiso
Club in Amsterdam, where following the gig, Rick sustained an ankle
injury under mysterious circumstances. When they returned to Air
Studios, he was often absent due to session commitments, leaving
the other four to lay down the tracks with his parts later overdubbed.
Rumours circulated regarding his extracurricular activities and Cousins
recalls a chance meeting with David Bowie's manager Tony Defries in
London's Speakeasy club where the latter claimed, 'We're going to take
your piano player away'.

Although Rick didn't receive a writing credit on *From the Witchwood,*
he did put forward a song, but in Cousins' view, there were too many

chord changes for the band to master. He also claimed the lyrics were incompatible with the chord sequence making it impossible to sing, even though Cousins, Hooper, and future Strawb Dave Lambert – who was visiting the studio – tried. The song was eventually abandoned, and Rick was bitterly disappointed. In *The Caped Crusader* biography, Cousins shared his forthright views with author Dan Wooding:

> Rick's songs at the time were dreadful. They just didn't make it. As a piano player and interpreter, there was no one better. I still maintain that he is the best keyboard interpreter of anybody's songs that I have ever heard. He's really exceptionally fluid. But, at the time, his own personal creativity wasn't too hot. He was inventive melodically, but his lyrics were pretty grim.

In *Yes: The Authorised Biography* by Dan Hedges published in 1981, Rick gave his view of events:

> I was too bogged down with my own ideas. I don't want to sound egotistical, but I suppose the Strawbs weren't enough of a musical challenge anymore. Because of the way the band was run, I knew there was no place for those ideas.

Mounting tensions in the Strawbs camp were fuelled by rumours that Rick was leaving and there were also disagreements over the material – they couldn't even decide which song to release as a single. Despite this, the resulting album was better than anyone could reasonably expect.

True to the title, 'A Glimpse of Heaven' is graced with a suitably reverential arrangement with celestial organ and the so-called 'Choir and Congregation of Air Strawb'. This was the singers in the band – basically everyone except Rick – overdubbed multiple times to create the sound of a massed choir. The words are some of Cousins's most poetic, painting evocative images of a pastoral landscape. The song really comes alive during the instrumental bridge with Rick's punchy organ underpinned by Cousins' banjo. It remains one of Rick's favourite Strawbs songs, which he also performed on *The Piano Album* released in 1995. Musically, the atmospheric 'Witchwood' harks back to mediaeval times with a layering of voices, electric and acoustic backing, and a rare outing for Rick's clarinet. Cousins' singing is at his most restrained telling of the mysterious witchwood, which 'Started singing with a strange unearthly sound'.

The mellow 'Thirty Days' is John Ford's debut song on a Strawbs album and it's a decent one. His voice has a lilt in comparison with George Harrison, complemented by Richard Hudson's distinctive sitar embellishments and soloing. Hudson's own composition 'Flight' is another mellow offering with an unmistakable Beatles influence, especially via the lush, wavering harmonies. Like on Ford's song, there seems little to occupy Rick, although he does contribute some lively piano to the rousing outro, which owes a conspicuous debt to 'Hey Jude'.

No Strawbs album would be complete without a moody Cousins mini-epic and here, 'The Hangman and the Papist' fills that role. The song was inspired by the sectarian troubles in Northern Ireland that were ever present in the early 1970s. From the opening bars, Rick cuts to the chase with a fuzzed organ break and the four-part harmonies are superb. It reaches an intense peak with a stately bolero riff similar to Ennio Morricone's music in the 1960s for Spaghetti western showdowns, especially *The Good, the Bad and the Ugly*.

Launching side two, 'Sheep' opens with a spiralling riff before motoring along with a chugging organ-embellished rhythm. Cousins' singing is positively manic as he laments the plight of the unfortunate titular animal on its way to the abattoir. Although Rick was disappointed by his organ playing on 'Sheep', he gives the subject the requisite bite before the song concludes with a serene vocal coda. Hudson's second offering, 'Canon Dale' is another laidback affair, although the heavenly harmonies lift it above the ordinary. During the instrumental bridge, sitar once again raises its psychedelic head.

For 'The Shepherd's Song', Mellotron and Moog make their debut on a Strawbs album. The former provides a shimmering backdrop to rippling piano, while the latter is responsible for the trumpet-like parps that accompany Cousins' flamenco-style acoustic guitar chords. It was inspired by Cousins' all-time favourite song, 'Alone Again Or' by Love and once again, he is at his poetic best, telling of a romantic encounter between two lovers in a rural setting. Driven by Hudson and Ford's muscular bolero rhythm, it builds to a majestic finale before the fade.

Following the drama of the previous song, the penultimate 'In Amongst the Roses' is a tranquil interlude that tells of a young girl gathering flowers in an abandoned garden. The soothing harmonies have a Crosby, Stills & Nash resonance with a light dusting of acoustic guitars. Hooper takes over lead vocals for the memorable 'I'll Carry on Beside You' and he's augmented for the stirring chorus. The song provides a suitably anthemic conclusion to the album, although the title is a tad ironic given the events that would soon follow.

Following the recording of *From the Witchwood*, Strawbs took a well-earned break in Italy, although a planned appearance at a festival in Rimini on the Adriatic coast was aborted when their gear, which travelled overland with the roadcrew, failed to arrive on time.

The album was launched with an appearance on BBC TV's weekly *Top of the Pops*, which was screened on Thursday evenings to a viewing audience of fifteen million at its peak in the 1970s. The show had recently introduced an album spot to reflect the popularity of LPs, and *The Yes Album* was also featured in the early part of 1971. Strawbs performed – or rather mimed to a pre-recorded track – 'The Hangman and the Papist' and Rick 'played' the organ with a paint roller which somewhat undermined the sombre nature of Cousins' song, much to his annoyance.

Not long after, Cousins received a telephone call from Strawbs' manager Mike Dolan who explained that he had had a meeting with Yes' manager Brian Lane and that Rick had left Strawbs. He had been offered £50 a week, almost double what he was earning with Strawbs. While Cousins bore no grudge, he was upset that Rick had not informed him personally.

From the Witchwood spent two weeks in the UK album chart, reaching a high of 39 on 17 July 1971, and sold 46,000 copies domestically. It was Strawbs' second release in America and although it failed to chart, it received a positive response, including their first album review in *Rolling Stone* magazine in November 1971.

Session musician extraordinaire

Rick's band hopping was not the only activity that occupied his time in 1971. Prior to the Yes offer, he had planned to form his own quartet and although this was never realised, they recorded two songs co-written by Rick and Dave Lambert – 'Coat of Many Colours' and 'Whirlwind' – for the film *Zee and Co*. It starred Elizabeth Taylor and Michael Caine, and was released in January 1972 to lukewarm reviews. To your author's knowledge, these songs have never received an official release.

Meanwhile, Rick's career as a session musician continued at a pace. Although he had already featured on hundreds of recordings, his best-known work as a keyboardist and arranger for hire was recorded and released in 1971. In 2004, Rick acknowledged to author Martin Popoff:

I was very fortunate to play on probably two of the most recognisable piano pieces – 'Morning Has Broken' and 'Life on Mars?' – and to arrange both of those. Now, the interesting thing is, if it hadn't been for Cat Stevens wanting to do 'Morning Has Broken' and Bowie writing 'Life on Mars?', then it wouldn't have helped people to recognise the way I play. So, I have a great debt of gratitude to both David Bowie and Yusuf Islam – or Cat Stevens – a great gratitude. And it was an amazing time!

For Cat Stevens' fifth album *Teaser and the Firecat*, Rick recorded the legendary piano arrangement for 'Morning Has Broken' at Morgan Studios, London, in March 1971. Despite a lovely vocal melody, it would have been a much lesser song without Rick's – uncredited – florid piano fills and embellishments. Adapted from a traditional hymn, when it was released as a single in January 1972, it became a top ten hit in many countries.

Around the same period, Rick played Hammond organ on Elton John's *Madman Across the Water* album on three tracks, including the title song. Although Elton is an adept organ player as he had proved earlier in his career as session musician Reginald Dwight, the piano remained his instrument of choice. In March 2022, Rick explained to Nick Krewen of the *Toronto Star*:

Elton's lovely, a great writer and a great piano player. People sometimes forget how great a piano player he is, but he hates playing the organ. Hates it … so I went into the studio and did the organ parts, which were great fun.

Although it's now regarded as one of his seminal albums, *Madman Across the Water* sold poorly when it was released in November 1971 and your author witnessed Elton and his band promoting the album in a half-empty De Montfort Hall in Leicester. In contrast, T. Rex – led by Marc Bolan – were the most popular pop group in the UK in 1971 and the album *Electric Warrior* was the year's best-selling. It was producer Tony Visconti who brought Rick onboard to play the piano glissandos on 'Get It On', a single hit Stateside in 1971, as well as being a UK number one. The glissando technique, often heard in blues and jazz jams, simply involves sliding the fingernails down the length of the keyboard. The story goes that Rick was £8 short of paying his rent at the time and was grateful when Visconti offered him £9 to play on the session.

27

Work on David Bowie's *Hunky Dory* album followed, which was recorded on and off during the summer of 1971 and just made into the shops in time for Christmas. When Bowie first played him the demos, Rick described them as: 'The finest selection of songs I have ever heard in one sitting in my entire life'. The album marked a turning point in Bowie's career and spawned two international hit singles, 'Changes' released in January 1972 and 'Life on Mars?' in June 1973. Rick was allowed a freehand with 'Life on Mars?' and the other musicians played around his piano arrangement. A third song from the album 'Oh! You Pretty Things' was a hit for Herman's Hermits' singer Peter Noone in 1971. In the book *David Bowie: A Life*, co-producer and engineer Ken Scott said of Bowie: 'The way he allowed Rick Wakeman to become a virtuoso on *Hunky Dory* was masterful. Other people would have smothered him. David knew what was best for him.' Musician Dave Stewart also enthused: '*Hunky Dory* just blew me away, especially the work that Rick Wakeman did on it. I learned every song on that album because they were so instructive'.

Rick's playing is pivotal to *Hunky Dory*. On the original LP sleeve, he is credited as 'Richard Wakeman on piano' in the handwritten notes where Bowie also modestly states 'I played some guitar, saxophones and the less complicated piano parts (inability)'. In the opening song 'Changes', Rick's playing is relatively lowkey for the verses, but he's into his rhythmic stride for the infectious chorus. Thanks to Scott's crisp production, the piano sound is sharp and clearly defined in the mix. Bowie's own 'less complicated piano parts are evident during the next two songs 'Oh! You Pretty Things' and 'Eight Line Poem' where his playing is hesitant, almost improvised. Along with a stirring orchestral arrangement, Rick is back on board for 'Life on Mars?', one of the most exhilarating songs of the 1970s. His tastefully melodic lines give way to pounding chords to accompany guitarist Mick Ronson's soaring solo during the instrumental breaks.

Side one concludes with the breezy 'Kooks' and the folky 'Quicksand', which both feature Bowie's jangly acoustic twelve-string to the fore. During the former, he combines with Rick's honky-tonk piano to superb effect and during the latter, double-tracked vocal harmonies and fluid piano fills float on a sea of strings. Opening side two, 'Fill Your Heart' finds Rick's jaunty piano lines vying with sax, strings, and Bowie's theatrical vocal for attention. At 2:35, Rick plays a brief but nicely judged descending blues run, which he repeats at the end of the song. He takes time out during both 'Andy Warhol' and 'Queen Bitch' but sandwiched in-between, 'Song for Bob Dylan' features some typically inspired piano chords and harmonies. Guitars and violin appear to be the only accompaniment on the final song, 'The Bewlay Brothers'.

Rick had worked for Elton John's producer Gus Dudgeon on numerous occasions, including Bowie's 'Space Oddity'. Dudgeon enlisted his services once again for the album *You Well-Meaning Brought Me Here* providing piano and organ for Ralph McTell. Rick's bread and butter, however, was pop singles for a fee of £12 a session. According to the programme notes for the *An Evening with Rick Wakeman* tour in 2000, he performed on ten of the top thirty UK singles during one week in 1971. Your author recalls that three of those were in the top ten. In March 2022, he claimed: 'In a five-year period, I did over 2,000 sessions of different sorts, some of which were amazing to do; some of which you scratched your head and went, 'Did somebody pay for this?' One album that Rick played on in 1971 may have easily disappeared without trace had it not been for his involvement.

Piano Vibrations

Personnel:
Rick Wakeman: grand piano
John Schroeder: orchestra
Chris: vocals
Produced at Pye Studios, London by John Schroeder
Release date: 1971
Record label: Polydor
Highest chart places: Did not chart
Running time: 32:45
Side one: 1. Take Me to the Pilot (3:00) (Elton John, Bernie Taupin), 2. Yellow Man (2:36) (Randy Newman), 3. Cast Your Fate to the Wind (2:35) (Vince Guaraldi, Carel Werber), 4. Gloria, Gloria (3:08) (John Schroeder, Anthony King), 5. Your Song (3:45) (John, Taupin). Side two: 1. Delta Lady (3:26) (Leon Russell), 2. A Picture of You (2:59) (Schroeder, King), 3. Home Sweet Oklahoma (3:22) (Russell), 4. Fire and Rain (3:25) (James Taylor), 5. Classical Gas (2:56) (Mason Williams)

Recorded at Pye Studios near London's Marble Arch and released in late 1971, *Piano Vibrations* is often credited as Rick's first solo album even though, at the time, it was just another session. Although the recording dates are undocumented, it would have been in his pre-Yes phase while still a member of Strawbs. His name is absent from the front cover of the original album sleeve; only on subsequent reissues with different artwork was 'Rick Wakeman' added. He does get a mention on the back of the original sleeve and on the LP label with the credit 'Featuring Rick Wakeman, Piano' along with 'Chris, who sang some of the songs'.

If Rick's fans anticipated a rock album, the words 'Easy Listening' on the original UK sleeve would have told them otherwise. *Piano Vibrations* features cover versions of popular songs arranged by Lew Warburton, who regularly contributed to various artist's compilations. Rick is backed by an orchestra directed by producer John Schroeder who wrote several hit songs in the 1960s. Schroeder produced a succession of easy-listening albums for Polydor in the same series, including *Latin Variations* and *Dylan Variations*. In *The Caped Crusader* biography, he explained:

> It was *Piano Vibrations* that enabled me to use Rick as a soloist. I knew from previous experience that as a musician, he was outstanding; his technique and feeling in his playing was superb. I thought he was a great talent who ought to be brought to the light in his own right and not lost forever on the session circuit.

Although the music and arrangements may be a far cry from Rick's more familiar style, it does showcase his talents as a pianist and his flair for improvisation. This is evident on the opening song 'Take Me to the Pilot', which is arranged in a swing jazz style with Rick's right hand pounding those top keys with a rare intensity. Another highlight is 'Cast Your Fate to the Wind' and although Rick has occasionally confessed his indifference to jazz, his performance on this instrumental standard is stunning at times.

Many of the tracks feature vocals – both male lead and female choir – where piano is often relegated to playing harmony and rhythmic chords. The two tracks co-composed by Schroeder are sugar-sweet instrumentals which find Rick in rare cocktail bar mode where the piano is all but swamped by strings. The second of these, 'A Picture of You', does feature a lively organ break, although it's not known if this is played by Rick.

Mention should also go to the unknown session guitarist who lays down some fine blues guitar fills, and spars superbly with the piano during a funky 'Home Sweet Oklahoma'. The same song features soulful singing and to my ears, 'Chris' is a euphemism for several different singers that feature across the album. The closing instrumental 'Classical Gas' boasts a spirited arrangement, but the piano is overwhelmed by the combined weight of brass, strings, and a metronomic drum pattern.

Although *Piano Vibrations* became a regular seller during the 1970s on the strength of Rick's popularity, he received no royalties. Like all his session work, he was paid a flat fee, telling author Dan Wooding: 'I just got a fee of £36 for four sessions it took to make the album. But I am still glad to have been able to make the disc – it gave me invaluable experience'. When the subject of *Piano Vibrations* has cropped up in more recent interviews, Rick has been less kind and is usually inclined to disown the album. Although it has its MOR tendencies and the rigid arrangements mean his playing is hamstrung at times, it does have its moments. Even so, it pales in comparison with the flamboyant touch Rick brings to his solo piano albums of more recent times.

Yes Come Calling

In *The Caped Crusader* biography, Rick related this entertaining account of how he was approached by bassist Chris Squire to join Yes following *The Yes Album* tour in July 1971:

I had been doing lots of sessions and was lying in bed after doing a three-day stint with about six hours of sleep. And that was typical. I had just arrived home, having had no sleep again and fell into bed. It was one of those things where the minute my head hit the pillow, I fell asleep. It felt so good, and then the phone rang. I Couldn't believe it, I covered my ear holes up and Ros, my wife, picked up the phone. I could hear the conversation. 'He's only just come in. He hasn't been back for three days, you know, he's really tired'. I was awake by then and let me tell you, I was furious! 'Gimme that phone'. 'Who's that?' And this voice said, 'Oh, hello, it's Chris Squire from Yes'. It's three in the morning, mind you, and he said, 'How are you?' I said, 'You phone me up at three in the morning to ask me how I am?'

Nonetheless, Rick was persuaded by Yes' manager Brian Lane to go along to a rehearsal in London's Shepherd Market and from that productive first session, 'Heart of the Sunrise' and 'Roundabout' evolved. In truth, the framework for both songs had already been worked out, but Rick added instrumental colour and texture to the arrangements that his predecessor Tony Kaye was either unwilling or unable to provide.

Like Rick, Kaye had studied at the Royal College of Music and by his own admission, he was content playing piano and his Hammond B-3 organ and didn't feel the desire to adopt modern keyboard technology. Kaye also liked to party and unlike his Yes colleagues who had family commitments, he took full advantage of the nocturnal distractions during the band's first tour of America in June and July 1971 supporting Jethro Tull.

When Squire and singer Jon Anderson visited Kaye's London apartment in August 1971 to deliver the bad news, it came as an unexpected blow, just as it had been for original Yes guitarist Peter Banks fifteen months earlier. Not for nothing was Anderson dubbed at the time 'the hippy with the iron hand' by the press. Kaye's last performance with Yes was at the Crystal Palace Bowl on 31 July 1971, where they were billed as Elton John's 'Special guest stars' ahead of four other bands. Looking back 50 years later, Kaye told *Prog* magazine:

> Being in a band is sometimes like being in a family, you know, you're living cheek by jowl, especially in the early days of the group, and plenty of bands have had problems dealing with each other, possibly because it is that family thing... it's true they (Mellotron and Moog) were not my favourite instruments.

Tellingly, when Kaye returned to the Yes fold in 1983 for the *90125* album, it was Trevor Rabin – who was more familiar with computerised technology – that provided most of the keyboards.

Prior to the offer to join Yes, Rick had already decided to leave Strawbs for artistic and financial reasons. He no longer felt he could offer anything creatively and he could earn far more as a full-time session musician than the weekly wage he was receiving as a Strawb. He also turned down a potentially lucrative offer from David Bowie to become part of the backing band he was forming for a forthcoming concept album and tour. *The Rise and Fall of Ziggy Stardust and the Spiders from Mars* was released in June 1972 and although uncredited, Rick did play the harpsichord on one song – the soulful 'It Ain't Easy' – which closed side one of the vinyl LP.

Rick chose Yes in preference to Bowie, believing that it was a band where he could contribute to the music as an equal. Also, life as a freelance session musician was no bed of roses, affecting his health and home life, particularly as his wife Rosaline was pregnant with their first son Oliver. Yes' star was very much in the ascendancy and as a full-time member, the financial stability would enable him to scale back the session work. Their previous LP – *The Yes Album* – had breached the UK top five on 20 March 1971 and spent 34 weeks in the charts. It also entered the American *Billboard* top 50. Yes' quasi-orchestral aspirations would also benefit from the addition of a versatile keyboardist.

At the beginning of 1971, Yes had been anything but solvent and *The Yes Album* was their make-or-break album as far as their record label Atlantic were concerned. Original manager and nightclub owner Roy Flynn had also been replaced by the wheeling and dealing Brain Lane – real name Harvey Freed – who set about promoting the band and putting their financial house in order. *Melody Maker* broke the news of Rick's inauguration on 21 August with the front-page headline 'New Yes Man'. He was quoted as saying:

The truth is that I found that I could offer more to Yes musically and they could offer me more because I found that I had reached my peak within the Strawbs. I think the Strawbs had got as far as they could with the present line-up, and the change will help them to move in a new direction.

Yes was not the only band to upgrade its line-up. Phil Collins and Steve Hackett had recently joined Genesis and in the years that followed, both bands and their individual members would compete with the likes of Emerson, Lake & Palmer, and Led Zeppelin to top the reader's polls in the UK music press.

Rick's departure was a severe blow to Cousins and for a while, he considered disbanding Strawbs. Following a spell in the country with a copy of the *I Ching* for company, he returned to London and resolved to continue. Ironically, it was following the recruitment of Rick's replacement, the talented Blue Weaver, that Strawbs really got into their progressive rock stride with the albums *Grave New World* in 1972 and *Bursting at the Seams* in 1973. The latter also spawned two UK hit singles. On *Grave New World*, the words to the song 'Tomorrow' are a thinly veiled dig at Rick following his remarks in an interview which had upset Cousins: 'You talked of me with acid tongue, and pointed trembling spiteful hands. Your presence almost overwhelmed'.

Coincidently, with history repeating itself as it so often does, in 2009, Rick's eldest son Oliver played keyboards for a reformed Strawbs before leaving to join Yes. For Cousins, it was a case of lightning striking twice.

Yes – Fragile

Personnel:
Jon Anderson: lead & backing vocals, acoustic guitar on 'We Have Heaven'
Steve Howe: electric and acoustic guitars, backing vocals
Chris Squire: bass guitars, backing vocals, additional electric guitar
Rick Wakeman: Hammond organ, grand piano, RMI 368 Electra-Piano and Harpsichord, Mellotron, Minimoog synthesiser
Bill Bruford: drums, percussion
Produced at Advision Studios, London by Yes & Eddie Offord
Recording date: 11 August – 5 September 1971
Release date: UK: 26 November 1971, USA: 4 January 1972
Record label: Atlantic
Highest chart places: UK: 7, USA: 4, Canada: 6
Running time: 40:28
Side one: 1. Roundabout (8:29) (Jon Anderson, Steve Howe), 2. Cans and Brahms (extracts from Brahms' 4th Symphony in E Minor, Third Movement) (1:35), 3. We Have Heaven (1:30) (Anderson), 4. South Side of the Sky (8:04) (Anderson, Chris Squire). Side two: 1. Five Percent for Nothing (0:35) (Bill Bruford), 2. Long Distance Runaround (3:33) (Anderson), 3. The Fish (Schindleria Praematurus) (2:35) (Squire), 4. Mood for a Day (2:57) (Howe), 5. Heart of the Sunrise (10:34) (Anderson, Squire, Bruford)

For the previous album, Yes had got it together in the country at a Devonshire farmhouse but, as Bill Bruford put it, their fourth album 'gestated loudly' in an upstairs room in Shepherd Market in London's Mayfair district. *Fragile* was originally conceived as a double album with studio recordings supplemented by a live disc of unrecorded stage songs, including 'America'. The idea was dropped, however, to accommodate the four-week recording deadline. With engineer and co-producer Eddie Offord behind the sixteen-track recording desk at Advision Studios in the heart of London, they often laboured from mid-afternoon into the early hours of the following morning. Like Yes, Offord was a rising star in the London music scene, and he was also the engineer of choice for Emerson, Lake & Palmer.

Yes' method of writing and recording was a revelation for their new keyboardist. In Strawbs, Dave Cousins would usually bring a complete song to rehearsal and the rest of the band would contribute to the arrangement. In contrast, the material for *Fragile* was mostly constructed in the studio in sections, with each musician contributing fragments such as a riff, a chord progression, a rhythm pattern, a verse, a chorus and so on. True, Jon Anderson often brought the words and the semblance of a melody to the table, but the songs would be deconstructed, allowing the four musicians within the band to make their contributions. It was manna from heaven for an aspiring musician and in Rick's own words: 'I thought this was absolutely fantastic!'

Although the band boasted several songwriters, Yes' melodies are often slight. The key to the songs is the way they're inventively structured and elaborately textured and embellished. When interviewed for *Classic Rock* magazine in 2020, guitarist Steve Howe explained: 'What Yes did was take simplistic things and complicate them a little bit, for our own amusement. Sometimes we'd take the chords out and just play riffs'.

Fragile is bookended by two of the band's best-known and – up to that point – longest songs, 'Roundabout' and 'Heart of the Sunrise'. When 'Roundabout' was released as a single edit in America in January 1972, it became a staple of FM commercial radio and was pivotal in turning young Americans onto the sound of Yes. 'Heart of the Sunrise' is Yes at their progressive best and their first song to break the ten-minute barrier. It provided the template for later epics like 'Close to the Edge' in the way that it skilfully builds tension followed by release – the song's payoff.

The four 'group' songs on *Fragile* are supplemented by five – mostly – solo contributions. These were allegedly incorporated due to the restrictions imposed by the tight recording schedule. It was Bruford who came up with the novel idea where each band member would take charge of an individual track with the other four performing as backing musicians under his direction. The plan backfired, however, when Rick, Anderson and Howe saw this as an opportunity to indulge in their own solo statements. Only Bruford, and to some extent Chris Squire, remained true to the drummer's original intent. As a result, Rick plays on six of the album's nine tracks.

Although it would become the encore of choice that never fails to get the Yes faithful on their feet, there are few album openers as effective as 'Roundabout'. In four distinct parts, it begins with a sustained piano chord which was recorded and played backwards so that it rises sharply in pitch rather than fades. It's swiftly followed by Howe's acoustic solo, which has a classical flavour despite being played on a steel – as opposed to nylon – strung guitar. When 'Roundabout' gets into its up-tempo, syncopated stride, the acoustic rhythm guitar has a harp-like timbre, doubled by Squire's signature Rickenbacker 4001 rumble, which is an octave lower. It demonstrated that popular music could both rock and be complex at the same time.

The lyrics were inspired by a journey from Aberdeen to Glasgow where the band's van negotiated several roundabouts and passed by lakes with the surrounding mountains appearing from the low cloud cover. They were also looking forward to returning home to their loved ones: 'Twenty-four before my love and you'll see I'll be there with you'. Rick plays organ for the most part and his rippling arpeggios, along with Howe's strummed riff, underpin Anderson's infectious chorus. During the 'Along the drifting cloud' middle-eight, the sharp organ stabs at 4:00 build the tension to fever pitch. Following a mellow acoustic guitar and vocal interlude, Rick's grandstanding Hammond solo at 5:50 blows away any lingering memories of his predecessor.

Around the time Yes were recording *Fragile*, Argent was working on their third album *All Together Now* on the other side of Regent's Park in Abbey Road Studios. The anthemic lead song 'Hold Your Head Up' features Rod Argent's dazzling Hammond workout that Rick would later cite as the finest organ solo of all time.

Rick's solo track has the unenviable task of following the barnstorming opener and was born out of necessity. As a former member of Strawbs, he was by default contracted to A&M Records with Rondor Music as his publisher, whereas Yes were signed to Atlantic with their own publishing arm, Yessongs Ltd. As a result of the conflicts of interest, Rick was prevented from contributing compositionally to *Fragile*. Instead, he opts for an interpretation of the 'Third Movement' from Brahms' 4th Symphony in E Minor' using six electric piano tracks, four organ parts, two harpsichord tracks and one Moog. The electronic soundscapes of Walter – later Wendy – Carlos are clearly an influence. Even at a little over a minute and a half, it was labour intensive as he overdubbed each segment while listening to the previously recorded part on headphones, resulting in the title 'Cans and Brahms'. Rick was later dismissive of his efforts, and it is perhaps overly ambitious when a piano solo, for example might have been less demanding and potentially more rewarding.

Anderson's equally brief 'We Have Heaven' Is another multi-layered offering, although it is arguably more successful. A door slams and running footsteps segue into the howling winds and bleak landscape of 'South Side of the Sky', one of Yes' most underrated songs. Due to the elaborate structure, it wasn't performed on stage in its entirety until the *Full Circle Tour* in 2002 following Rick's return to the fold.

Bruford's syncopated drum volley leads the charge, joined by angular guitar, jagged bass lines and rhythmic organ chords. Beginning at 2:07, Rick's inventive piano solo provides the song's centrepiece, joined by wordless counterpoint harmonies courtesy of Anderson, Squire and Howe. It remains one of Rick's best performances on a Yes album and is a masterful display of technique, precision, and restraint. From 5:40, it's a white-knuckle ride led by Howe's demonic playing and the cascading guitar part at 6:30 that follows the line 'The river can disregard the cost' is inspired. The song's subject of nature and mankind in conflict and turmoil is reflected in Roger Dean's debut sleeve artwork for Yes. On the inner booklet, a mountain climber is scaling a vertical precipice and on the front cover, a spacecraft sails over a miniature, seemingly idyllic world which explodes into fragments on the reverse. Steve Howe commented in the *Classic Rock & Prog* Yes special in 2021:

...We didn't design it, but we kind of adapted Roger's works into our music. It's amazing how tight the two entities are. ...They were special times because, although we didn't know it, it became harder and harder to create that kind of environment.

Although 'South Side of the Sky' is not an obvious song to cover, contemporary American prog bands Spock's Beard and Glass Hammer did an excellent job in 2002 and 2007, on the *Snow* Limited Edition and *Culture of Ascent* albums, respectively. It's almost inconceivable that Rick didn't receive a writing credit, but the legal complications between record labels and publishers dictated otherwise. A resigned Rick said to *Classic Rock* magazine some 50 years later:

You didn't stop to fight about it with management because that would have held things up, and you were so keen just being there. They said it would all get sorted out and I'd get my writing credits, but I never did.

Side two of the vinyl LP opens with the shortest track, Bruford's instrumental 'Five Percent for Nothing', which signposts the jazz rock route he would later follow. Rick's contribution to the track is minimal, providing the spiky organ chords.

In the early stages, 'Long Distance Runaround' had a working title, 'Corporal Salt', because it reminded the band of a song on *Sgt. Pepper*. Bruford's beat displacement gives the song an off-kilter feel which is perhaps apt given that the lyrics reflect the frustrated recollections of a relationship that went sour. The agile instrumental hook is superbly performed by double-tracked guitars, while rhythmic piano and hi-hat underpin the vocal melody. At a single friendly three and a half minutes, it was the B side to the 'Roundabout' single and would prove to be one of Yes' most durable stage songs, acting as an introduction to 'The Fish'. Squire's contribution would also enjoy longevity as a stage favourite until his untimely death in 2015. Speaking to *Prog* magazine some years later, Rick acknowledged the Yes rhythm partnership:

> Bill was fantastic and worked so closely with Chris Squire. They argued fiercely, but…I don't think I've ever worked with a drum, bass combination quite as incredible as Bill and Chris. The outcome was just always sensational.

Although the simplest to record, Howe's classical guitar meditation 'Mood for a Day' is arguably the most successful of the album's solo contributions.

'Heart of the Sunrise' remains a firm favourite with fans and the band, especially Rick. It's also the first Yes song to fully showcase the wide range of keyboard colours and textures that would become synonymous with the band and Rick. The opening bass riff is in 6/4 time and the frantic, King Crimson style rhythm patterns during the intro were aptly described by Anderson to Yes biographer Dan Hedges as 'Schizoid'. Howe cuts loose with his beloved Gibson ES175D punctuated by Rick's dissonant organ chords. At 0:40, rising Mellotron strings create an air of anticipation and as the song progresses, Bruford swings in 6/8, 9/8 and 10/8 time. Around the 6:52 mark, it has a Mahavishnu Orchestra moment with a jazzy sequence incorporating frantic call-and-response synth bursts which Anderson later attributed to the influence of Stravinsky. A short piano motif is introduced at 8:04 – proceeding the 'Straight light moving and removing' verse – which is later taken up by organ and guitar. At 9:23, Mellotron returns, joined by Moog, to sweep the song to its grand finale.

The lyrics explore several themes and to begin with, the message is love and following your heart's desires. Anderson welcomes the dawning of a new day but also reflects on the loneliness people often feel when lost in a big city. Anderson's poetic words are complemented by the orchestrations with Moog embellishments and Mellotron string washes. Rick brought the techniques of his classical training to Yes, including recapitulation and thematic variations. This is very much in evidence in 'Heart of the Sunrise' and would blossom with 'Close to the Edge'. When interviewed for *The Guitar Magazine* in 1992, Howe looked back on *Fragile*:

> It's clever how Rick's influence showed a lot on that album with what we called the 'Rick-recapitulation' bit where we would go back and play fragments of previous segments interspersed with Rick's piano.

Guitar had overshadowed keyboards on *The Yes Album*, but Rick brought stiff competition and as such, Howe had to up his game. There were now four virtuosos in the band and it's no coincidence that *Fragile*, *Close to the Edge* and *Tales from Topographic Oceans* all feature some of Howe's most colourful and inventive guitar work. Rick was later quoted in *Prog* magazine:

> Steve played guitar like nobody else I've ever known. He just had a completely different sound to everybody I'd ever played with... It left a lot of gaps for me to put in and do things, which was fantastic.... It was like, I suppose, five architects in the same room trying to build one amazing building.

Fragile entered the UK chart at number seven on 4 December and it was the first of a successful chart run on both sides of the Atlantic as well as mainland Europe and Australia. Following its release in America in January 1972, *Fragile* had staying power and remained in the *Billboard* top 100 chart well into mid-summer, peaking at number four in May, eventually achieving double Platinum status. Critics on both sides of the Atlantic were equally bowled over and reviews were unanimously positive. In a radio interview in Sydney, Australia, in 1977, Rick confirmed his verdict of *Fragile*:

Magic, a fantastic album. I've always said that. It really is a great album…it has all the ingredients…I was allowed the freedom to use quite a few keyboards. It was quite incredible because I could suddenly do all the things that were bottling up inside for years. When those sorts of things happen and they come out, it's very fresh.

In *Time and a Word: The Yes Story* by Martin Popoff, he said of his first experience of working with Yes and the band's other new discovery:

Fragile was a wonderful album to record. The record company left us alone. The management left us alone. In fact, everybody left us alone to produce what we wanted. That was a wonderful time. It happened on *Close to the Edge* as well. It doesn't happen too much these days. And it was the first time working with Roger Dean. Steve discovered Roger, I believe, and introduced him and his work to us. We were all mightily impressed, and Roger became a really important part of the Yes family.

Dean's artwork also graces the eight-page booklet inside the sleeve with a page dedicated to each band member. Rick opts for a long list of acknowledgements along with a photo of himself and his pet dog Becky.

In 2004, *Fragile* was given some unexpected exposure on the big screen in the comedy film *School of Rock*. A wannabe music teacher played by Jack Black hands a copy of the CD to a young student and says: 'Yes, that's the name of the band. Listen to the keyboard solo on 'Roundabout'. It will blow the classical music out your butt!'

With *Fragile* in the can, Yes rehearsed for a week in South Molton, Devon before setting off on a five-week UK tour. One of Rick's first stage appearance with Yes was on 30 September at the De Montfort Hall in Leicester, a venue frequented by your author in the 1970s. At the beginning of November, they embarked on the band's second trip to America and Rick's first. They doubled their earnings from the previous visit thanks to *The Yes Album* scaling the *Billboard* chart and a single version of 'Your Move' receiving regular airplay. Nonetheless, they were still the opening act for bands as diverse as Procol Harum, King Crimson, Ten Years After and the J. Geils Band. They also shared the bill with Emerson, Lake & Palmer on several occasions, a dream package for prog fans.

In November, while they were in Los Angeles, Rick and manager Brian Lane met with Jerry Moss, head of A&M Records and agreed a solo recording deal which included an advance of $12,500 for the first album. After the final show in New Orleans on 18 December, Yes returned home for the 1971 Christmas holidays but would be back on the road soon after the festivities ended.

1971 was not only a productive year for Rick, it was also 'Rock's Golden Year' according to author David Hepworth. The Rolling Stones unleashed *Sticky Fingers*, The Who responded with probably their finest hour, *Who's Next*, while Rod Stewart believed that *Every Picture Tells a Story*. Like Yes, Jethro Tull were getting into their progressive stride with *Aqualung*, joined by ELP with *Tarkus* and Genesis with *Nursery Cryme*. *Every Good Boy Deserves Favour* proved The Moody Blues were still at the forefront of symphonic rock while Pink Floyd experimented with *Meddle*. Heavy metal also ruled as evidenced by *Led Zeppelin IV*, Black Sabbath's *Master of Reality* and Deep Purple's *Fireball*. On the other side of the Atlantic, the Doors released Jim Morrison's swansong *L.A. Woman*, the Beach Boys declared *Surf's Up*, and Harry Nilsson scored with *Nilsson Schmilsson*. Marvin Gaye took soul to a new level with *What's Going On*, Joni Mitchell was feeling *Blue*, and Carole King embroidered her masterpiece *Tapestry*.

1972 - Close to Perfection

The first four records from Yes were all practice runs for the fifth – the killer – *Close to the Edge.*
Bill Bruford – *Bill Bruford: The Autobiography* published in 2009.

Rick had proven to be an instant hit with Yes fans, and he knew how to court the members of the press who warmed to his easy-going personality. They shared the same watering holes, and the additional publicity certainly didn't do the band any harm even though compared with Rick's alcohol consumption, his colleagues were virtually teetotal. Although Yes were a tight-knit working unit, they didn't have the same social relationship that was part and parcel of being a Strawb and later, a member of Rick's own band. When interviewed by Penny Valentine for *Sounds* in 1972, Rick admitted:

It's not been an easy band to slide into because we don't really mix socially – which is good really because I don't think music and social life mix very well. I mean, we all argue after gigs anyway. The first time I met them, I couldn't believe a group could argue so much. I thought we were about to split up and thought, 'Oh well, there's £100 and a job out the window'. But then I found they just argue, everyone tells everyone else when they think they've played badly on a gig. They're all total individuals.

In terms of touring, 1972 would prove to be a particularly busy – and demanding – year for Yes and Rick. With concert tickets in the UK in the early 1970s roughly a third of the price of a vinyl LP, tours often ran at a loss to promote the latest album, which was the real money spinner. How times have changed. To advertise the *Fragile* tour dates, the 'Yes' pre-Roger Dean speech bubble logo, which dates back to 1969, was still in use. It's also evident from Yes bootlegs recorded in January 1972 that the setlist included a keyboard solo from Rick based on 'Temperament of Mind'.

Before Yes business resumed, Rick and Steve Howe took time out to guest on Lou Reed's eponymous debut album, which rather surprisingly was recorded in London rather than New York. When *Lou Reed* was released in April, it was poorly received and is perhaps best remembered for Tom Adams' superb cover artwork. The classic

Transformer album produced by David Bowie and Mick Ronson would follow just six months later. Rick also played piano on the album *Writer of Songs* by folk singer and songwriter Harvey Andrews.

On 14 and 15 January, Yes made their debut appearance at London's recently opened Rainbow Theatre before heading off to Belgium and the Netherlands. They returned to the UK for three dates and found time to check into Advision Studios with producer Eddie Offord during the first two days in February to record 'America' and prepare for the next album. Rick, along with members of Yes, also made a tentative start on his debut solo album at London's Trident Studios on 10 February, although it would be another year before its eventual release.

Yes' ten-and-a-half-minute version of Simon & Garfunkel's classic 'America' surfaced the following month on the budget-priced sampler album *The New Age of Atlantic*. Previously unreleased tracks from Led Zeppelin and Yes bookend the album and helped nudge it to number 25 in the UK chart on 25 March. Despite the proximity of the recordings, 'America' is unlike anything on *Close to the Edge*, even allowing for the fact that it's a cover version. Paul Simon's search for his homeland is deconstructed and rebuilt, incorporating a lengthy instrumental jam and a nod to Leonard Bernstein's 'America' – a favourite of The Nice. Yes had been performing 'America' live as a showcase for Howe and Kaye's guitar and organ soloing but was dropped from the setlist when Rick joined. This studio version really swings with expansive organ and Mellotron while Howe's rampaging guitar solo channels his inner Duane Eddy. Appropriately, on 17 July, an edited 'America' was released as a single in its namesake country and received regular airplay on FM radio.

Following the London recordings, there was little time for rest before Yes headed off for a six-week coast-to-coast tour of the USA which opened in New York on 14 February. To coincide, *Fragile* and the 'Roundabout' single were released in January. Even in its truncated form, the latter was smart, and it rocked, attributes that appealed to young Americans who sent it to number thirteen on the *Billboard* chart. It was Yes' first bona fide hit and until 'Owner of a Lonely Heart' in 1983, 'Roundabout' remained their signature song in America. The band's hard work continued to reap rewards; both *Fragile* and *The Yes Album* achieved gold disc status in America around this time. Yes supported Black Sabbath during the tour and Rick developed a firm friendship with the West Midlands hard rockers. In 2015, Black Sabbath drummer Bill Ward confirmed to author Martin Popoff:

On that tour we were the headliners. Kinda strange to say that but yeah, we were the headliners. Good tour; we had Rick Wakeman with us all the time. Nice guy, great musician – that's why he ended up on so many of our records. We were always with Rick. He'd travel with us; he'd be on our bus, or he'd be on our plane. 'Oh, Rick Wakeman again' (laughs).

Ward's recollections regarding Rick's involvement on Black Sabbath's records are exaggerated, although to be fair, the 1970s was the drummer's heavy drinking period. Rick played on just the one album – *Sabbath Bloody Sabbath* in 1973 – adding piano and Minimoog to the song 'Sabbra Cadabra'. Ward may have been getting confused with long-serving Sabbath keyboardist Geoff Nicholls. Ward also gave Yes a glowing endorsement:

Great band; they're the best. They've left some very high-quality music. If you're a student of music, then go listen to Yes, because the quality and the level of musicianship is brilliant, and it comes together very well. And Jon's lyrics are very pleasing because it's coming from a strong place and he's talking about humanness, which is what makes the world turn around. So Yes is a very important band, brilliant.

Rick was not the only member of Yes to forge bonds during the American tour. On the final date, the 27 March, Yes shared the bill with King Crimson in Boston where Bill Bruford received an offer from Robert Fripp he couldn't refuse. Unbeknown to everyone at the time, possibly even Bruford himself, it would be his final gig with Yes until the *Union* tour some nineteen years later.

Rick was by now dubbed 'The Wizard of Yes' by the music press which put him under extreme pressure to deliver the goods every night. As a result, he suffered from nerves each time he took to the stage during the tour. He was also plagued with equipment problems from his five-keyboard set-up. The following year in February 1973, he confessed to journalist Chris Welch:

I worry about my music. I have to keep on top of it all the time. Music has become so much more important to me, and everything has to be just right. Sometimes I get into a trance from playing and the more perfect things become the more I get involved.

Although it was Rick's second trip across the Atlantic, he was awestruck by the vastness of North America. On 26 February, he missed the birth of his first son Oliver as Yes were performing in New Jersey that night. Anderson, Squire, Kaye, and Alan White would eventually relocate to the USA but Rick, like Howe and Bruford, remained on home soil. He was a tax exile in Switzerland in the late 1970s and he moved to the Isle of Man in the 1990s, but since 2005, he has lived in rural South Norfolk in the east of England.

It's not hard to speculate that Rick's increasing reliance on presentation including multiple stacked keyboards and flamboyant stage wear was his way of combating stage fright. There were also false rumours circulating that he was about to leave the band which put a strain on the relationship with his colleagues, particularly self-appointed band leader Jon Anderson. Encouraged by producer Eddie Offord, the other members of Yes, especially Howe, were jumping on the health food bandwagon, but Rick stuck to his regular diet of meat and beer.

To pass the time during the lengthy travelling between gigs, Rick had picked up several books on the previous USA tour, including *The Private Life of Henry VIII* by Nancy Brysson Morrison, first published in 1964. The chronicle of the authoritarian king and his unfortunate six wives struck a chord with the keyboardist and when Yes returned to London at the end of March, he spent several days in the studio during April developing the concept. The album would feature members of Yes, Strawbs and the cream of London's session musicians. In *The Caped Crusader* biography, Rick confirmed:

I would record a couple of tracks, go out on tour with Yes, and when I came back and listened to the tapes they never sounded right. So, I would do it over again and change it. It went on like that.

When Rick announced to the press that he was working on a solo album, his prediction that it would be in the shops by July proved to be a tad optimistic. He also had other matters to deal with. Earlier in the year, Yes' accountant David Moss advised Rick that due to the healthy income from *Fragile*, he needed to offset his tax liability. As a result, in April, he and Ros moved from their modest dwelling in West Harrow to a mansion-sized property in Gerrards Cross, Buckinghamshire, situated 20 miles to the west of central London. The following month, he bought a Rolls Royce Silver Cloud. In the *Say Yes!* autobiography Rick proclaimed: 'My apprenticeship course completed, I was now a fully-fledged rock star!' His rock star talents would be put to the test on his second Yes album, which would become their masterpiece.

Journalist Derek Jewell – who presented the Saturday night progressive rock and jazz programme *Sounds Interesting* on BBC Radio 3 – visited Advision Studios during the recording of *Close to the Edge*. In an article titled 'Yes and the coming of age' published on 16 July in *The Sunday Times*, he described the scene:

Rick Wakeman, musician with Yes, sits in a studio recording the group's fifth album. Seven keyboard instruments surround him – piano, organ, electric piano, electric harpsichord, two Moog synthesizers and a Mellotron, which can create orchestral sounds of strings, woodwind and brass, in any key, in any combination, from instrumental tapes it contains.

Signs like 'controllers', 'oscillator bank', 'modifiers' litter the electric instruments, which can be combined cunningly by a small digital computer. The music may be fragile and very beautiful; sometimes, it suggests several symphony orchestras, an artillery barrage and Dantean screams.

Wakeman began studying piano at five, later studied at the Royal College of Music, and is now, early twentyish, a master musician. The creative flair and technical mastery required of him are staggering; enough, perhaps, to make many symphony orchestra section members quail.

Yes – Close to the Edge

Personnel:
Jon Anderson: lead vocals
Steve Howe: guitar, electric sitar, backing vocals
Chris Squire: bass, backing vocals
Rick Wakeman: keyboards
Bill Bruford: drums, percussion
Produced at Advision Studios, London by Eddie Offord & Yes
Recording date: June – July 1972
Release date: 13 September 1972
Record label: Atlantic
Highest chart places: UK: 4, USA: 3, Canada: 7
Running time: 37:45

Side one: Close to the Edge (18:50) (Jon Anderson, Steve Howe): i. The Solid Time of Change, ii. Total Mass Retain, iii. I Get Up, I Get Down, iv. Seasons of Man. Side two: 1. And You and I (10:09) (Anderson, Howe, Bill Bruford, Chris Squire): i. Cord of Life, ii. Eclipse, iii. The Preacher, the Teacher, iv. Apocalypse, 2. Siberian Khatru (8:57) (Anderson, Howe, Rick Wakeman)

In May, rehearsals for the fifth Yes album got underway at the Una Billings School of Dance in Shepherds Bush, West London. Bill Bruford later recalled that the mirrors that covered the walls reflected the sound back at deafening high volumes. Coincidently, parts of Genesis' 'Supper's Ready' – which rivals 'Close to the Edge' as the definitive prog rock epic – was written and rehearsed in the same venue in the summer of 1972.

Recording began on 1 June in the familiar surrounds of Advision Studios, but it would be an arduous process that would take them through to the middle of July when the equally painstaking mixing began, supervised by Eddie Offord. Advision had become a second home for Yes, where Offord would often find himself competing with the band members – especially Chris Squire – for a seat at the recording console and hands on the faders.

The title track was a mammoth undertaking which was recorded onto sixteen-track tape in short sections and then spliced together. There were also multiple overdubs of vocals and instruments, and it was only when the piece was complete that the band was able to rehearse and perform it from start to finish. Seemingly, only Jon Anderson and Steve Howe, as the principal architects, could visualise the piece from the outset.

The recording of 'Close to the Edge' has often been described by the band members themselves and others witnessing the process, including author Chris Welch, as five individuals contributing to a large sonic jigsaw. Like parts of *Fragile* before it, 'Close to the Edge' was not so much written as constructed in the studio with each band member pitching in to embellish Anderson and Howe's initial words, melodies, and riffs.

Anderson described 'Close to the Edge' as a spiritual quest of self-realisation and a search for the inner divine, with Hermann Hesse's 1922 novel of self-discovery *Siddhartha* an inspiration. The 'river' figures prominently in both Hesse's and Yes' writing as seemingly a metaphor for life, although it can also be interpreted to represent a spiritual

47

journey of enlightenment. Coincidentally – or otherwise – the 1973 album *Photos of Ghosts* by Italian prog-maestros PFM opens with the song 'River of Life' with words penned by former King Crimson lyricist Peter Sinfield.

Close to the Edge pre-emps *Tales from Topographic Oceans* and not just because it contains a side-long song. The lyrics to both albums are spiritual and mystical and full of symbolism and have in common keywords like 'movement' and 'revealing' while 'sun' – Anderson's metaphor for God – dates back to *Fragile*. At the time, he summed up *Close to the Edge* in relation to its predecessor to journalist Tony Stewart of the *New Musical Express*:

> *Fragile* was the situation of the band at the time. ...The whole idea of the band at the time was very fragile; it could collapse. And as it happened, it's taken off and got better and better. Now we're close to the edge of spiritual awareness within the framework of the group, making music.... We're close to the edge of making music that might stand up in a few years' time.

The singer had been expanding his intellectual horizons, soaking up inspiration from literature and classical music, including Sibelius and Stravinsky, who he described to biographer Dan Hedges as '...The kings of early twentieth-century music'. The title track also brings Hector Berlioz's *Symphonie Fantastique* to mind, and possibly under Rick's influence, they were also dabbling in the Sonata form. The musical structure of exposition, development, and recapitulation, along with an introduction and a coda, had been hinted at in the group songs on the *Fragile* album, but on 'Close to the Edge' especially, the form is more fully developed. Anderson also cited the symphonic structures of Dvorak, Holst, and Tchaikovsky as inspiration, while the orchestral sweep of Sibelius' *Symphony No. 5* is most apparent in 'And You and I' that opens side two.

When interviewed by author Will Romano for his book *Close to the Edge: How Yes' Masterpiece Defined Prog Rock* published in 2017, Anderson reflected on the freedom they were granted by Atlantic Records:

> It was like a blessing to be able to go into the studio and create and not have anybody tell you what to do. And that was happening in the early 1970s. In a way we were free to do what we wanted and were

capable enough to create a certain kind of music, and at the time, professional enough to know when to stop, because all you wanted to do then was to take it on the road and perform it on stage.

Rather than connecting several unrelated songs – as bands are prone to do in extended works – 'Close to the Edge' is a fully contained piece with recurring melodies that build tension and release. While it's undeniably rock music with elements of jazz – the dissonant instrumental intro – and folk – the pastoral mid-section – it closely follows the classical model of variation, changing the tempo, texture, and tone to create different moods and emotional responses from the listener.

Bookended by the synthetic sound of twittering birds, a flowing stream, and swirling electronics, it bursts into life with a frantic guitar-led jam that alternates between D major and D minor with synth going into overdrive. At 2:48, Bruford's rimshot snare introduces 'The Solid Time of Change' and the principal theme which is underpinned by majestic organ chords and synth fills. The uplifting chorus during 'Total Mass Retain' is supported by Mellotron stabs and Moog followed by Rick's call and response Hammond lines that subside into 'I Get Up, I Get Down'. Waler Carlos' *Sonic Seasonings* influenced the dreamy intro featuring sitar, synth and Mellotron washes and at 9:47, Rick's electric piano pulse underpins the counterpoint, three-part harmonies.

Not surprisingly, the instrumental sequence beginning at 12.12 is Rick's favourite. The majestic St Giles-without-Cripplegate church organ is usurped by a Minimoog fanfare where traditional and contemporary attitudes to organised religion collide. The final sequence, 'Seasons of Man,' begins with an atonal variation of the main theme driven by Squire's pumping bass line and atonal synth. At 14.50, it takes timeout for a stunning Hammond solo before racing headlong to the triumphant vocal finale 'On the hill we viewed the silence of the valley …' on a wave of Mellotron strings. Although Rick acknowledged Anderson as the band's prime mover and songwriter, his playing, and arrangements throughout are indispensable. His mastery of keyboard technology, classical training and virtuoso technique gave the songs a symphonic opulence that Anderson had been striving for since forming Yes four years earlier.

Opening side two, 'And You and I' is another four-part masterpiece. By Anderson's own interpretation, the song is a critique of self-serving politicians who pursue their own quest for power rather than the needs of those that elected them. It opens tentatively with 12-string acoustic guitar followed by a lyrical Minimoog figure that weaves its way through 'Cord of Life', joined by Anderson's wistful alto – tenor. In the 'Eclipse' sequence at 3:40, the combination of Moog, Mellotron strings and pedal steel guitar is Yes at their majestic best. In the folky 'The Preacher, the Teacher', Anderson is seemingly referring to the inner teacher or inner self, while the line 'Sad preacher nailed upon the coloured door of time' is possibly a reference to the crucifixion. 'The Apocalypse' is a suitably grandstanding finale complete with upward sweeping Minimoog lines and thundering piano chords.

Following the grandeur of 'And You and I' and 'Close to the Edge', Yes remind us that they are still a rock band at heart with 'Siberian Khatru'. Rick receives his first compositional credit on a Yes album, co-writing the themes while Anderson is responsible for the lyrics. In the *New Musical Express* in 1972, the singer confessed:

A lot of my words get abstract because I can't concentrate on one storyline. The 'Siberian Khatru' track is just a lot of interesting sounding words, although it does relate to dreams of clear summer days. The title means winter, but it's meant to be the opposite. It doesn't really mean a great deal.

Even so, Yes fans have spent many an hour debating the meaning behind the songs, especially the line 'Gold stainless nail'. Anderson also believed he devised the word 'Khatru' but later discovered that it was Yemeni for 'As you wish'. Nonetheless, for their sonic value alone, his abstract world play works superbly within the context of 'Siberian Khatru'. Squire and Bruford unite for a powerhouse performance – for the final time on a Yes studio album – underpinning Howe's infectious riff supported by Rick's rhythmic organ fills. Anderson's multi-tracked vocals glide over the top and at 3:15, Rick's spirited harpsichord solo has a distinct baroque flavour. It was played on a traditional instrument brought to the studio by manufacturer Thomas Goff who also advised how it should be miked. This solo was the principal reason for Rick receiving a writing credit. The extended instrumental payoff is prefaced by Anderson's stream of conscious couplets, including 'Bluetail, tailfly', sweetened by Mellotron strings and flute.

For his second Yes album sleeve, Roger Dean introduced the iconic snake-like logo that's still in use to this day. The plain green – Chris Squire's favourite colour – cover gives no hint of the splendour of the inner artwork depicting a lake atop a plateau with waterfalls cascading on all sides. Its music and imagery are in perfect harmony and Dean's panoramic scene reflects the expansive nature of Yes' music.

Close to the Edge spent nine weeks in the UK top 20, reaching number four on 30 September. On the same date, it was certified gold in America. In a review in November, *Rolling Stone* magazine made this perceptive observation which could be applied to progressive rock in general:

> If there's a problem involved in placing or defining Yes' music, it's a direct result of our establishing rigid criteria and admitting only which qualifies, rather than expanding our own border of perception in accordance with what artists choose to present.

Musical Drum Stools

In his autobiography published in 2009, Bill Bruford commented:

> *Close to the Edge* was completed and it was a huge hit, but, more importantly, it remains a classic of the genre. I don't understand how we managed it, but somehow, we got lucky. To this day, it seems to have the perfect form, and form is everything. Maybe it was karma for all the grief we had gone through during the first three or four years. I loved the record, hated making it, and was immediately certain I would never try to do that again.

Bruford is essentially a spontaneous drummer and the long, drawn-out recording sessions, which often dragged on into the early hours of the morning, was not something he wanted to repeat. When he announced during the mixing of the album that he was leaving Yes, it was a bombshell that devastated his colleagues, including Rick. The drummer and keyboardist, who were born just one day apart, had established a mutual respect for each other's professionalism, even though Bruford, unlike Rick, was a jazz man at heart. Although Bruford was the third of the founding members to exit Yes, he had the distinction of being the first to jump ship rather than being cast adrift. He later explained in his autobiography:

> I'd only played with a handful of people in my short four-and-a-half years as a musician, and I knew that what I was after was not to be

found in my current position, despite the rocket-fuelled start to my career that the band had given me. I loved Yes, but I thirsted to learn more, and I was ready to change the world with King Crimson.

With a world tour to promote *Close to the Edge* looming, Yes needed a capable replacement fast, and they found one in the shape of Alan White, drummer with Joe Cocker's touring band. A couple of weeks earlier, he had sat in during a rehearsal when they played 'Siberian Khatru', so they were very aware of his talents. At the time, he was living in Eddie Offord's apartment in Victoria, London and it was the producer who introduced White to Yes. He came with the kudos of being a former member of John Lennon's Plastic Ono Band and having played on the *Imagine* album. Since the late 1960s, he had been a much-in-demand drummer, building up an impressive CV with the likes of George Harrison, Ginger Baker's Airforce, Alan Price, and Terry Reid. As I was writing this section of the book, he sadly passed away unexpectedly on 26 May 2022 and many well-known musicians from the rock world played tribute.

To his credit, White learnt the entire Yes set in three days before his debut appearance in Dallas, Texas, on 30 July. Driven by nervous energy, he performed brilliantly, although he was less successful over the subsequent two weeks as he found his way within the band. Rick acknowledged his initial concerns to journalist Chris Welch in February 1973:

When Bill suddenly left, I couldn't believe it. I thought the band would crumble. For the first time, I had started to feel part of the band and then it seemed it was about to end. When Alan White came in, I was really worried because it had taken a year for me to settle in. But Alan was great and worked really hard.

Shortly before the Yes tour, Rick rekindled his relationship with a former bandmate. Recorded at The Manor Studio in Oxfordshire in June 1972, *Two Weeks Last Summer* was Dave Cousins' debut solo album. The stellar cast of musicians includes Dave Lambert (guitar), Jon Hiseman (drums), Roger Glover (bass) and Rick (organ, piano). It was originally released in the UK and Italy only in October 1972, selling around 5,000 copies. In his autobiography, Cousins recalls Rick's contribution:

That evening Rick drove up to The Manor in a Rolls Royce – it felt a bit strange, as it was the first time we had played together since he left Strawbs. On 'Ways and Means', he played what I believe to be the best (piano) solo of his career. In fact, he played several, each one different and each one as good as the other. However, it was 'Blue Angel' that gave Rick a problem. The third part of the song has just two chords, but they change at irregular places to fit the lyric. In the end, I had to stand in front of him at the organ and raise my left hand for D and my right for Emaj7. In the end, it sounded wonderful, and I was delighted that we had re-cemented our relationship.

The *Close to the Edge* tour was long but rewarding, both financially and artistically, and cemented Yes' reputation as one of the finest and most popular live acts of the 1970s. Although the three-dimensional stage sets would not appear until the following tour, there were several innovations. Based on the mirror ball principle, lighting technician Michael Tait designed and built a rotating disc that reflected beams of light into the audience during the intro and outro of 'Close to the Edge'. During the 'I Get Up, I Get Down' midsection, subdued lighting and billowing dry ice tumbling off the front of the stage evoked Roger Dean's artwork. To ensure a pristine sound to match their studio recordings, Eddie Offord joined them on the road with a state-of-the-art mixing console and a 7,000-watt stereo PA system. He utilised backing tapes for the complex 'Close to the Edge' as he explained to author Will Romano:

I had two tape machines, there were church organs, and there would be vocal parts and even sound effects and a lot of instrumental parts that they couldn't do live. I would be there cueing in these church organ parts, and Rick would actually be kind of miming to some of them, you know? So, it was really a major kind of production.

Rick embarked on the tour fully equipped, including two Minimoogs, two Mellotron 400s – one with strings, brass and woodwind and the other with choir, vibes and sound effects, a Hammond C3 organ, an RMI electric piano and harpsichord and a baby grand piano which was raised off the floor so that he could play it standing up. With his stacked battery of instruments, Rick was able to faithfully reproduce the studio symphonics of *Fragile* and *Close to the Edge*, particularly when playing the Moog and Mellotron in tandem. As they had done on the *Fragile* tour, Yes entered the stage to the stirring strains of the finale of Stravinsky's 'Firebird Suite' which, thanks to Mellotron strings, segues seamlessly into the opening bars of 'Siberian Khatru'. Rick's solo spot included excerpts from *The Six Wives of Henry VIII* with the addition of flashing lights, sound effects and smoke providing a visual and aural highlight.

On their previous American jaunts, Yes supported several local and UK bands, but on the *Close to the Edge* tour, they were the headliners. Regular opening act, Eagles, entertained the crowd with their recent hits 'Take It Easy' and 'Witchy Woman'. Admission at the time would have set you back between $5 and $6, compared with UK ticket prices which were little more than £1.

Yes returned to the UK for a headlining appearance at London's open-air Crystal Palace Bowl on 2 September. They were supported by an eclectic array of acts, including Lindisfarne, Wright's Wonderwheel and the underrated Capability Brown with Mahavishnu Orchestra, a band much admired by Yes, billed as guest stars from the USA. Yes' performance was marred by problems with the PA system and Rick's keyboards caused by interference from a BBC power transmitter. While acknowledging the sound issues, Jerry Gilbert gave Alan White's British stage debut with Yes a positive review in *Sounds* with the headline 'Superb Palace'.

In the *Melody Maker* poll awards later that month, Rick was elbowed into second place by Keith Emerson in the world's best keyboard player category. The following year, Rick was voted number one, which would establish the trend for the rest of the decade. Although they had ample competition, Rick and Keith established themselves as the foremost keyboard pioneers of the 1970s. Emerson admittedly had a head start; he had recorded five albums with The Nice and three with ELP prior to Rick joining Yes.

Following the Crystal Palace gig, Yes played a handful of further UK dates before embarking on a three-month hike across the length and breadth of the USA and Canada. The gruelling tour schedule was not in vain; *Close to the Edge* breached the top ten in the UK, USA and Canadian album charts between September and November 1972. Unusually for Yes, a performance at the Coliseum in Indianapolis on 20 September was stopped two songs into the set due to crowd problems caused by heavy-handed police tactics.

During a three-week break in October, Rick returned to the UK to put the finishing touches to his concept album for release the following January. He also appeared on BBC TV's weekly rock show *The Old Grey Whistle Test* on 24 October, where he discussed the album with presenter Bob Harris and previewed 'Catherine of Aragon'.

Back in America on 19 November, Rick met designer Denise Gandrup who made the famous sequined cape – the first of many he would wear on stage. Seven of the final Yes shows performed in North America in 1972 were recorded and released in 2015 as the fourteen-CD *Progeny: Seven Shows from Seventy-Two*. Sonically, the recordings are a general improvement over the *Yessongs* live album, and the performances demonstrate the consistency and precision Yes were able to maintain across successive nights on tour. There are however variations in Rick's solo performances of 'Excerpts from The Six Wives of Henry VIII' with subtle improvisation between the set pieces.

On 9 December, Lou Reizner's production of The Who's rock opera *Tommy* featuring the London Symphony Orchestra and a stellar cast of singers was staged at London's Rainbow Theatre. Rick was part of the pick-up band that augmented the orchestra and he approached Reizner to discuss plans for an ambitious stage production of his own. *Tommy* had originally been scheduled for the Royal Albert Hall but fell victim to the venue's ban on rock concerts imposed in March of that year. The unruly behaviour of audiences was blamed, but the ban was short lived and repealed in 1973.

The following week, Rick returned to the Rainbow with Yes, ending the year as they began with back-to-back shows at the theatre on the 15 and 16 December. On this occasion, they were filmed, and the resulting footage was released in cinemas in 1975 and made the top 50 list of highest-grossing films of the year. The 73-minute *Yessongs* film was released on video in 1991 and later DVD. On both nights, Yes were supported by Tony Kaye's new band Badger whose performance was also recorded – but not filmed – resulting in the *One Live Badger* album co-produced by Jon Anderson and released in 1973.

If Yes were at the peak of their powers, they were at the tip of a creative year for progressive rock. Snapping at their heels was Genesis' *Foxtrot*, Emerson, Lake & Palmer's *Trilogy*, Gentle Giant's *Octopus*, Wishbone Ash's *Argus,* and Jethro Tull's *Thick as a Brick*. The latter was number one in several countries, as was *Seventh Sojourn*, The Moody Blues' final album, for more than five years. Prog didn't have it all its own way; there was a plethora of milestone releases across the rock spectrum, including *Talking Book* by Stevie Wonder, *Harvest* by Neil Young, *Exile on Main St.* by the Rolling Stones, *The Grand Wazoo* by Frank Zappa, *Can't Buy a Thrill* by Steely Dan, *Caravanserai* by Santana, Roxy Music's debut and David Bowie's *The Rise and Fall of Ziggy Stardust* to name just a few.

1973 - Tales from the Tudor Court

> I had to make it instrumental because my lyrics are appalling. I can
> sing in tune, but my voice is not that good.
> Rick, interviewed by Rosalind Russell for *Disc* magazine, in late
> 1972, prior to the release of *The Six Wives of Henry VIII*.

1973 was a prolific year for Yes, releasing an unprecedented five LPs
worth of music. Ironically, there was a vinyl shortage that year due to a
global oil crisis, although sales were seemingly unaffected. The year got
off to a bad start when it was reported in January that £3,500 worth of
equipment, including two of Rick's Minimoogs had been stolen over the
Christmas holiday. The *Close to the Edge* tour resumed on 8 March with
their first visit to Japan and Australia, although three proposed dates
in New Zealand were cancelled. In April, they were in more familiar
territory in the southern States of the USA. With a proposed visit to
South America in May also cancelled, Yes would be off the road for six
months, their longest break since the band's formation in 1968.

With Yes and solo activities keeping Rick busy, session work was
sparse in 1973, although in April, he did find time to guest on Al
Stewart's *Past, Present and Future* album. Recorded in London's Trident
Studios, it boasts a who's who line-up of musicians and he is just one of
six keyboard players featured. Three weeks into the year, Rick's long-
awaited debut album finally hit the record stores. Speaking to author
Martin Popoff in 2004, he recalled:

> I can thank David Bowie very much because David told me many years
> ago to write everything on the piano. He said, 'If you write it on the
> piano and it works as a piece of music, you can do anything with it'. He
> writes everything on a really horrible old 12-string guitar, and he says, 'If
> it sounds good on this, then I know it will sound good whatever I do; it
> can only get better and better'. And so, everything that I've ever written,
> I've done on the piano, and the great thing about that is that you can't
> get any more minimalist than when you're sitting at the piano.

Rick Wakeman - The Six Wives of Henry VIII
Personnel:
Rick Wakeman: Minimoogs, 400-D Mellotrons, Steinway 9' grand piano,
Hammond C3 organ, RMI electric piano, ARP synthesiser, harpsichord,

church organ, portative organ
Additional personnel:
Bill Bruford: drums on 'Catherine of Aragon' and 'Anne Boleyn'
Ray Cooper: percussion on 'Catherine of Aragon' and 'Anne Boleyn'
Dave Cousins: electric banjo on 'Catherine Howard'
Chas Cronk: bass guitar on 'Catherine Howard'
Barry de Souza: drums on 'Catherine Howard'
Dave Lambert: guitar on 'Catherine Howard'
Mike Egan: guitar on 'Catherine of Aragon', 'Anne of Cleves', 'Anne Boleyn' and 'Catherine Parr'
Steve Howe: guitar on 'Catherine of Aragon'
Chris Squire: bass guitar on 'Catherine of Aragon'
Alan White: drums on 'Anne of Cleves', 'Jane Seymour' and 'Catherine Parr'
Dave Wintour: bass guitar on 'Anne of Cleves' and 'Catherine Parr'
Les Hurdle: bass guitar on 'Catherine of Aragon' and 'Anne Boleyn'
Frank Ricotti: percussion on 'Anne of Cleves', 'Catherine Howard' and 'Catherine Parr'
Laura Lee: vocals on 'Anne Boleyn'
Sylvia McNeill: vocals on 'Anne Boleyn'
Judy Powell: vocals on 'Catherine of Aragon'
Barry St. John: vocals on 'Catherine of Aragon'
Liza Strike: vocals on 'Catherine of Aragon' and 'Anne Boleyn'
Produced at Morgan and Trident Studios, London by Rick Wakeman
Recording date: February – October 1972
Release date: 23 January 1973
Record label: A&M
Highest chart places: UK: 7, USA: 30, Australia: 9
Running time: 36:36
All tracks written by Rick Wakeman, except as noted otherwise
Side one: 1. Catherine of Aragon (3:45), 2. Anne of Cleves (7:50), 3. Catherine Howard (6:36). Side two: 1. Jane Seymour (4:46), 2. Anne Boleyn (The Day Thou Gavest Lord Hath Ended) (6:32) (Rick Wakeman, E. J. Hopkins), 3. Catherine Parr (7:00)

With Yes off the road in January, Rick was free to celebrate the long-awaited release of his debut solo album. The previous week on 16 January, he, along with old pals Dave Cousins and Chas Cronk, appeared on BBC TV's late-night rock show, *The Old Grey Whistle*

Test, to promote the album. They performed 'Catherine Howard' and it proved to be a significant boost for the album.

Although A&M Records had given Rick a healthy advance in November 1971 to kick start his solo career, they were less enthusiastic when they realised they had an instrumental album on their hands. The advance, along with his lucrative income from Yes, gave him the wherewithal to invest a good deal of time and money into the production and it shows in the finished recording. He's supported by a cast of eighteen, including members of Strawbs, Yes, and a host of musicians and vocalists familiar to Rick from his session work.

Rick fully immersed himself in the life of the 16th-century King of England and his ill-fated wives, providing the ideal subject for a concept album. With little experience in writing lyrics, Rick wisely avoided the song format and opted for six, mostly instrumental vignettes. Although this was not unique in rock music, it was considered a commercial risk at the time. It would also be the first of many 'themed' albums that Rick would record over the ensuing years.

Rick initially recorded at Trident Studios with engineer Ken Scott where they cut 'Catherine of Aragon'. Scott also worked on 'Anne Boleyn' but had to bow out due to other commitments. The album was completed at Morgan Studios with Paul Tregurtha who would continue to record with Rick up to, and including the *No Earthly Connection* album. The album was in the can by the end of September 1972, but Rick spent part of October remixing it.

Although the music has that recognisable Wakeman stamp, the individual tracks are musically diverse, intended to capture the personality of each of the six queens based on Rick's personal interpretations. It was an opportunity to exploit the array of keyboards he had at his fingertips with few concessions made to Renaissance music or the instrumentation of the period. Instead, he presents six musical portraits in a 20th-century setting.

For fans that had been lucky enough to witness Rick's solo spot on the *Close to the Edge* tour, some of the tunes may have already been familiar. Amongst an arsenal of analogue keyboards, the Minimoog features prominently and was many keyboardists' instrument of choice in the early 1970s. Although Rick utilised musicians he was familiar with, he was conscious that it should not sound like a surrogate Yes album. During the 'Catherine of Aragon' session, Rick, together with Steve Howe, Chris Squire, Bill Bruford, and percussionist Frank Ricotti, recorded a version of

George Bizet's 'Farandole' which was eventually released on *The Classical Connection 2* album in 1993, albeit misspelt as 'Farandol'. A piece was written for Henry, but it was omitted from the album due to the constraints of vinyl. Entitled 'Defender of the Faith', It eventually surfaced in its full ten-minute splendour on the 2009 live recording *The Six Wives of Henry VIII Live at Hampton Court Palace*. As early as 1973, Rick had planned to perform his debut work at Henry's royal palace but was turned down.

Critical reception for Rick's debut album was divided, as typified by these two reviews. Penny Valentine was gracious in her assessment in *Sounds*:

> The whole collection here and indeed the liner notes on the Queens complement each other very well. The album itself is a mix of the emotional flash, the calm and gentle, the grand and the simple. A good mixture. And while my own favourite is 'Jane Seymour', particularly because I have an affection for the sound of a beautiful church organ, I think this is an album that is both an excellent showcase for Wakeman and a well-presented musical work.

Steve Clarke was less enamoured in his review in *New Musical Express*:

> There are the seeds of some fine music here, but it's never allowed to grow or blossom out. Some of the trouble is probably due to the fact that there's no real vocal hooks to catch on to. The only vocals come from a choir who hum over a tapestry of acoustic guitar and piano, sounding like good cigarette advert material. The lack of colour, say by a guitar or horn, may also account for the loss of direction which, in my opinion, the album suffers from.

Arguably, dismissing an instrumental keyboard album for not having conventional singing and lead guitar – although it does – is rather like criticising an Indian restaurant for not serving egg and chips. When *The Six Wives* was released, 19-year-old Mike Oldfield was recording his mostly instrumental debut album *Tubular Bells,* which was unveiled four months later. Several record companies had rejected Oldfield's demos due to the absence of vocals and drums until the enterprising Virgin Records took him under their wing.

Like *Tubular Bells*, *The Six Wives* was a slow burner, entering the UK chart one month after the release date, where it peaked at number seven in the second week on 3 March. It spent 22 weeks in the top 100, not bad for an instrumental concept album. It not only launched Rick's solo career, but it was also an inspiration for other musicians – particularly his Yes colleagues – to later flex their musical muscles outside the confines of the band. It went on to become a multi-million global seller and remains one of Rick's most popular releases.

To add a note of levity to the subject, the cover artwork features a sepia-tinged photo of Rick striding past waxwork models of Henry and his wives on display at London's Madame Tussauds. On the back of the gatefold, there is a portrait of each wife accompanied by biographical notes. The inside spread features a studio photo of Rick encircled by his keyboards, with each one conveniently tagged.

The opening track began life as 'Handle with Care', which Rick had intended for his debut album with Yes. This was nixed for contractual reasons and was extensively reworked as 'Catherine of Aragon' with three musicians from *Fragile* appropriately lending their collective talents. Interviewed in 1975, Rick confirmed that this was the first track written and that musically, it is as much Henry's theme as it is Catherine's. She was Henry's first wife, noted for her brains rather than beauty and it was her shrewdness that kept her head on her shoulders, unlike some of her successors. Organ, guitar, and piano make a dramatic entrance before the latter takes up the memorable main theme, underpinned by articulate bass and thunderous timpani rolls. Rhapsodic piano is accompanied by acoustic guitar and a wordless female choir before organ, bass and drums return to bring the track to a triumphant conclusion. 'Catherine of Aragon' was regularly performed with the English Rock Ensemble in subsequent years and occasionally paired with 'Catherine Howard'.

Wife number four 'Anne of Cleves' was divorced soon after her marriage to make way for Catherine Howard, but fortunately, she also evaded the axeman. The track's freeform, jazz fusion style and varying time signatures, in Rick's opinion, reflected Anne's mental state. A spiralling electric piano motif launches into a frantic Hammond-led jam fest. At 3:30, there's a subliminal nod to the Latin jazz standard 'El Cumbanchero' written by Puerto Rican Rafael Hernández Marín in the 1940s. Crashing piano chords and Mike Egan's dissonant guitar solo have the final word before the whole thing finally runs out of steam. Alan White's muscular drumming is outstanding on this track which was his first studio recording after joining Yes.

The free-spirited 'Catherine Howard' was favoured by Henry until he discovered her extramarital indiscretions, and she was beheaded in 1542. Nonetheless, she has the strongest melody, and this is probably the album's best-known piece. During the session, Chas Cronk met Dave Cousins and joined Strawbs that same year. 'Catherine Howard' became a stage favourite in later years and was performed during the *Wakeman with Wakeman* tours in the early 1990s. Solo piano, joined by drums, bass, acoustic guitar and Mellotron introduce the main theme, which is recapitulated in several different settings. Cousins' electric banjo solo provides a respite before being overwhelmed by a strident Moog fanfare. A burst of honky tonk piano before the return of the main melody with Mellotron strings, piano arpeggios, and tubular bells. The final sequence with slowly fading Mellotron flute is suitably haunting.

Henry's third wife 'Jane Seymour' had a passive nature and gave him the son he so desperately desired, but the birth resulted in her own death, aged just 28. To reflect her personality, Rick chose the majestic timbre of the pipe organ at St Giles Church, Cripplegate, London. The mood is broken at 2:45 and 3:10 with irreverent Moog stabs to signify her tragic demise. This is another occasional live piece that has been performed solo, with the ERE and with an orchestra – most notably at London's Hampton Court Palace in May 2009.

'Anne Boleyn' alternates between fast and slow passages with fine rhythm support. The rich tones of the choir enter at 2:03, followed by a joyous piano-led theme which introduces two very different synth solos, one funky and the other strident. It develops into a jazz fusion workout with distorted minor chords. When Henry married his second wife, he unreasonably demanded a son, not the daughter Anne Boleyn gave birth to. Her reward for this, and her fiery temper, was execution in May 1536. The mood changes at 5:30 with a poignant grand piano and choir rendition of 'St Clement' – the music for the hymn 'The Day Thou Gavest Lord Hath Ended'. Prior to recording this sequence, Rick dreamt that he heard the hymn playing at Anne Boleyn's funeral service.

The final track is dedicated to the sixth wife, 'Catherine Parr'. She was level-headed and outlived Henry but died after bearing a child to her fourth husband, Thomas Seymour. Another stage favourite, this is a multi-part gem containing no less than eight separate sequences. A galloping organ theme sets the scene with an almost country and western groove. Mellotron choir features in two contrasting sections and at the three-minute mark, it hits its rock stride with a rhythmic Moog theme that glides into a tubular bells section. An ambient interlude with skyrocketing electronic effects and celestial organ is swept away by the simulated sounds of crashing waves. The opening theme is reprised, joined by double-tracked Moogs before the glorious sound of the Hammond C3 and rotating Leslie speaker brings the track and album to a satisfying close.

Rich Wakeman

Rick had joined Yes in 1971 on a salary of £50 a week, but as the money began to roll in from record sales and concerts, the band moved onto a percentage. On Brian Lane's advice, they invested in property and other assets that would appreciate in value. In addition to his house in Gerrards Cross, Rick acquired a farmhouse in Devon and invested in new equipment. He also built up an impressive 20-strong collection of classic cars, which included Rolls Royce's, Bentleys and his pride and joy, a 1957 Cadillac presented by Gerry Moss, head of A&M Records. The press reacted with the predictable headline in 1973 'Rich Wakeman'.

Yes – Yessongs

Personnel:
Jon Anderson: lead vocals
Chris Squire: bass guitar, backing vocals
Steve Howe: electric and acoustic guitars, backing vocals
Rick Wakeman: keyboards
Bill Bruford: drums on 'Perpetual Change' and 'Long Distance Runaround' / 'The Fish (Schindleria Praematurus)'
Alan White: drums on all other tracks
Recorded live in America, Canada and the Rainbow Theatre, London
Produced by Eddie Offord & Yes
Recording date: February – December 1972
Release date: 18 May 1973
Record label: Atlantic
Highest chart places: UK: 7, USA: 12, Canada: 8
Running time: 129:16
Side one: 1. Opening (excerpt from 'Firebird Suite') (3:45), 2. Siberian Khatru (8:50), 3. Heart of the Sunrise (11:26). Side two: 1. Perpetual Change (14:08), 2. And You and I (9:55). Side three: 1. Mood for a Day (2:52), 2. Excerpts from 'The Six Wives of Henry VIII' (6:35), 3. Roundabout (8:33). Side four: 1. I've Seen All Good People (7:00): a) Your Move, b) All Good People,

2. Long Distance Runaround / The Fish (13:45). Side five. Close to the Edge (18:41): i. The Solid Time of Change, ii. Total Mass Retain, iii. I Get Up I Get Down, iv. Seasons of Man. Side six: 1. Yours Is No Disgrace (14:21), 2. Starship Trooper (9:25): a) Life Seeker, b) Disillusion, c) 'Würm'

Several bands released their first live albums in 1973, including Genesis, Focus, Wishbone Ash, Uriah Heep, Hawkwind, Mahavishnu Orchestra and Yes. While live recordings appear with almost monotonous regularity in recent times, they were sporadic during the 1970s, with even the most popular acts averaging just one or two. It's a small wonder that bootlegs were so popular.

Partly because of the band's hectic touring schedule, almost fifteen months separated the release of *Close to the Edge* and *Tales from Topographic Oceans*, the longest between any two Yes studio albums thus far. The release of *Yessongs*, therefore, served two purposes; it bridged the gap to satisfy expectant fans, and it committed to vinyl their prowess as a formidable live act. With a wealth of material to choose from, *Yessongs* is spread across three LPs, following in the footsteps of the *Woodstock* soundtrack in 1970 and the Grateful Dead's *Europe '72* in 1972.

By 1972, songs from the *Yes* and *Time and a Word* albums had been dropped from the band's setlist and would not reappear until many years later. As such, *Yessongs* is a virtual rerun of the three most recent albums, with the songs re-sequenced to simulate the arc of a live concert. Amongst the omissions is 'South Side of the Sky', a song that even Yes found difficult to recreate live in the 1970s. Although Yes have a reputation for slavishly replicating their material on stage, *Yessongs* demonstrates otherwise. In some instances, the complex arrangements have additional introductions and endings, replacing the slow start or fade on the studio versions.

'Siberian Khatru' is a good example, a song that readily lends itself to live performances, becoming a regular show opener for years to come. The coda is a heady rush featuring staccato wordless harmonies where – unlike the studio version – Howe reprises the opening guitar phrase immediately before it comes to a sudden, and very impressive stop. It's effective and dynamic, enhanced by Anderson's pronounced 'Bop' at the end.

Even more striking is the opening to 'And You and I'. The studio version begins with Howe's 'OK?' remark to a recording engineer and hesitant strumming. Here, it explodes into life with the same majestic

Above: A thoughtful looking Yes plan their future shortly after Rick joined the band in 1971. The smiling Bill Bruford would unexpectedly leave the band the following year.

Right: Rick composed the majority of his solo material at home on the piano.

Left: Although Rick had already appeared on hundreds of session recordings, *Just a Collection of Antiques and Curios* was his first album as a fully-fledged member of a band. (*A & M*)

Right: Strawbs taking time out in 1970 at the London Apprentice pub by the River Thames. Rick greatly admired the songwriting talents of band leader Dave Cousins (center). (*A & M*)

Left: Rick was unable to persuade Cousins to include one of his own compositions on *From the Witchwood* and soon after the album's release in 1971, he left Strawbs. (*A & M*)

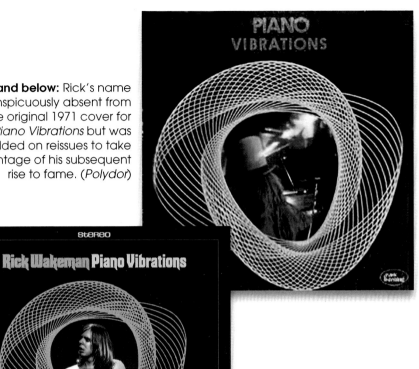

Right and below: Rick's name is conspicuously absent from the original 1971 cover for *Piano Vibrations* but was added on reissues to take advantage of his subsequent rise to fame. (*Polydor*)

Right: His substantial piano contributions to David Bowie's legendary 1971 album remain Rick's most significant work as a session musician. (*RCA*)

Left: Although he was denied a writing credit, Rick's creative input on his first album with Yes in 1971 elevated the band to new heights, particularly in North America. (*Atlantic*)

Right: For many, *Close to the Edge* released in 1972 is the quintessential progressive rock album and a landmark in both Yes and Rick's careers. (*Atlantic*)

Right: Rick's debut solo album confounded both the critics and his record label, but his growing legion of fans ensured its commercial success in 1973. (*A & M*)

Below: *The Six Wives of Henry VIII* album was a showcase for Rick's growing arsenal of keyboards as pictured on the inner gatefold sleeve. (*A & M*)

Right: Rick made several appearances on BBC TV's weekly rock show *The Old Grey Whistle Test* and on 24 October 1972, he was in conversation with presenter Bob Harris promoting the forthcoming album.

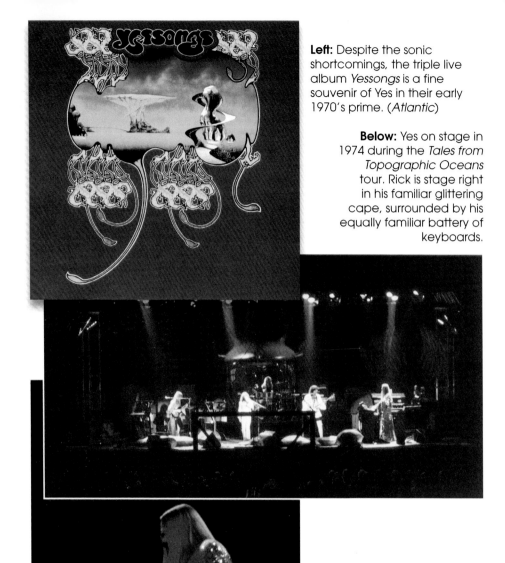

Left: Despite the sonic shortcomings, the triple live album *Yessongs* is a fine souvenir of Yes in their early 1970's prime. (*Atlantic*)

Below: Yes on stage in 1974 during the *Tales from Topographic Oceans* tour. Rick is stage right in his familiar glittering cape, surrounded by his equally familiar battery of keyboards.

Left: A front-row view of Rick putting the Minimoog through its paces. Although the tour was not a happy experience, he was the consummate musician during every performance.

Above: Roger Dean's iconic gatefold artwork for *Tales from Topographic Oceans*. One fish is clearly a different species to the other four, Rick perhaps? (*Atlantic*)

Above: Despite his misgivings about the album, Rick was positive about Yes' performance at Madison Square Garden when interviewed with Steve Howe for *The Old Grey Whistle Test* in February 1974.

Right: To keep the costs down, Rick's second solo album was recorded live in January 1974 although true to form, he staged a lavish production. (*A & M*)

Left: Album number three from Rick released in 1975 was another themed offering on a grand scale, complete with orchestra and choir. (*A & M*)

Right: Rick, band, and orchestra recreating *The Myths and Legends of King Arthur and the Knights of the Round Table* for the 9,000-strong audience at London's Empire Pool, Wembley in May 1975.

Left: Bassist Roger Newell playing the Wal custom triple neck guitar in 1975. Chris Squire played the same instrument on the 1977 *Going for the One* tour after Rick rejoined Yes.

Above: With no less than fourteen keyboards at his disposal, Rick is seen performing 'Guinevere' on grand piano at the Empire Pool, Wembley.

Left: The Empire Pool shows would be the last that English Rock Ensemble singer Gary Pickford-Hopkins performed with Rick.

Right: Rick totally immersed in the performance as *King Arthur* reaches its climax with 'The Last Battle'.

THE SOUNDTRACK ALBUM OF THE KEN RUSSELL FILM

LISZT○MANIA

MUSIC
PRODUCED AND
ARRANGED BY
RICK WAKEMAN

FILM
STARRING
ROGER DALTREY

Also Starring
SARA KESTELMAN
PAUL NICHOLAS and
FIONA LEWIS

Featuring Songs &
Performances by
ROGER DALTREY &
RICK WAKEMAN

Guest Stars
RINGO STARR
RICK WAKEMAN

A GOODTIMES ENTERPRISES
PRODUCTION
From Warner Bros.
A Warner Communications
Company

Left: In 1975, Rick's first foray into film soundtracks was a frustrating experience and he would revisit *Lisztomania* some 27 years later. (*A & M*)

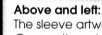

Above and left: The sleeve artwork for *No Earthly Connection* released in 1976 features a distorted image of Rick. It could only be viewed in its proper perspective when the sheet of reflective plastic supplied with the album was rolled into a tube and placed on the center of the image. (*A & M*)

Right: Rick's friend from his teens, singer Ashley Holt was a member of the English Rock Ensemble for three years before the line-up was disbanded following the *No Earthly Connection* tour.

Left: The ERE horn section of Reg Brooks and Martyn Shields in full swing at the Farnham Maltings during the UK tour on 27 April 1976.

Right: Rick warming to the audience – and the cameras - at the Farnham Maltings. The show was recorded by the BBC for *The Old Grey Whistle Test*.

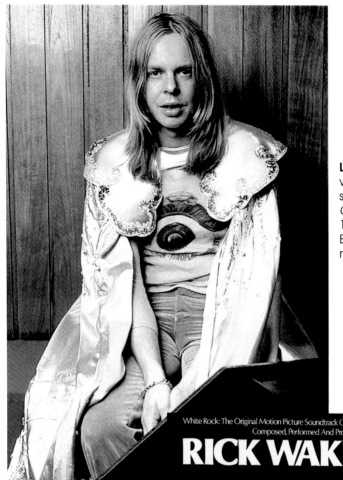

Left: A relaxed Rick waiting to take to the stage. The *No Earthly Connection* tour in 1976 was the first in Europe under his own name.

White Rock: The Original Motion Picture Soundtrack Of The Innsbruck Winter Olympics
Composed, Performed And Produced By

RICK WAKEMAN

PANAVISION _STEREO SOUND_

Right: Rick's second soundtrack album released in 1977 was a far more satisfying experience than the first and entered the UK top twenty. (*A & M*)

Right: Rick's return to Yes in late 1976 resulted in one of their most celebrated albums of the 1970s. (*Atlantic*)

Left: Rick teamed up with Squire and White again for his seventh solo album released in 1977. (*A & M*)

Right: Rick on stage with Chris Squire, Jon Anderson, Steve Howe and Alan White. The *Going for the One* tour in 1977 was one of Yes' most prestigious to date.

Left: Released in 1978, Yes' second album following Rick's return divided opinions, not least among the band members themselves. (*Atlantic*)

Right: Yes in matching bomber jackets and shades trying to look cool on the back of the *Tormato* album sleeve. (*Atlantic*)

Left: Rick watching Steve Howe intently as they perform on the groundbreaking revolving stage during the *Tormato* tour.

Right: Rick playing the Polymoog in the promotional video for the single release of 'Wonderous Stories'. It was a real buzz for Yes fans when it reached the UK top ten in October 1977.

Left: He is all at sea in the video for the single release of 'Don't Kill the Whale' which charted in the UK in September 1978.

Right: A video was also recorded for 'Madrigal' from the *Tormato* album with Rick suitably dressed in period costume for his harpsichord recital.

Left: Released in 1979, *Rhapsodies* was Rick's final album of the 1970s and his last for his record label A&M. (*A & M*)

Below: On the inner gatefold sleeve of *Rhapsodies*, Rick emulating *Superman: The Movie* which was a huge box office hit at the time. (*A & M*)

Left: Not released until 1980, Yes' second official live album features Rick on recordings from 1977 and 1978. (*Atlantic*)

pedal steel guitar, Mellotron and Moog theme that concludes the song. For practical reasons in the 1970s, Howe plays the 12-string acoustic part that follows on a double-neck electric guitar.

Rick's 'Excerpts from The Six Wives of Henry VIII' is a solo tour de force and although the source material has no connection with Yes, it went down a storm when played live. It opens with 'Catherine of Aragon' and at 1:16, piano plays a medley of silent movie themes resurrected from 'Temperament of Mind'. Following a brief return to 'Catherine of Aragon', at 2:43, Rick launches into Handel's 'Hallelujah Chorus', complete with Mellotron choir. At 3:53, 'Jane Seymour' – minus the church organ – is followed at 4:48 with a frantic burst of 'Catherine Howard'. The final minute is given over to simulated explosions, police and air raid sirens, and if you were there, smoke and flashing lights.

Although Steve Howe's soloing often dominates, Rick's input elsewhere on the album is considerable. Mellotron provides the bridge between the taped intro of Stravinsky's 'Firebird Suite' and 'Siberian Khatru' and *Yessongs* is an opportunity to hear his take on songs from *The Yes Album*. In 'Perpetual Change', Hammond organ and Mellotron strings make their mark during the extended instrumental jam. An equally lengthy 'Yours Is No Disgrace' opens with improvised honky tonk piano followed by sizzling organ and Moog volleys. This is Yes at their rawest and most unfettered. 'I've Seen All Good People' on the other hand, remains true to the spirit of the original with Mellotron replicating the sound of the recorder during 'Your Move' while organ gives Howe's guitar a run for its money during a storming 'All Good People'.

Both 'Heart of the Sunrise' and 'Close to the Edge' stay true to the studio versions and capture the same epic sweep. In the former, Mellotron strings hover ominously over Chris Squire's lead bass lines and Alan White's intricate drumming, while in the latter, Rick faithfully recreates the timbre of the pipe organ before unleashing his devastating Hammond solo. Following sprightly electric piano in 'Long Distance Runaround', Rick adds Mellotron to Squire's 'The Fish', accentuating Anderson's eight-syllable 'Schindleria Praematurus' choral finale.

A song that had yet to find its niche in the setlist is 'Roundabout'. When it was performed in later years as the encore, the mid-section was sometimes jettisoned to maintain the song's momentum, although, on *Yessongs*, it's fully intact. Here, the call-and-response guitar and organ exchanges that follow the organ solo are riveting. Likewise, although he didn't play on the studio version, Rick stamps his authority on 'Starship Trooper', particularly the 'Würm' finale. The guitar and synth sparring is classic Yes, guaranteed to bring the show to a dramatic close. It's also one of the few Yes songs Rick performed with his own band in later years.

Although sound-wise *Yessongs* is superior to the bootlegs that were flooding the market, at times, it's a sonic pea soup even though the remastered reissues in more recent times have gone some way to remedy the situation. Eddie Offord, who was responsible for the sound on the *Close to the Edge* tour, offered this explanation to Yes biographer Dan Hedges:

> I'd gotten so involved with the P.A. system that when it came to do a live album, I couldn't sit in the truck outside and sit in the hall at the same time. I didn't actually record most of that, though I have to say that I wasn't very happy with the quality of that album.

In contrast with Alan White's drum sound, Bill Bruford's sound on the two tracks recorded in February 1972 during the *Fragile* tour is relatively clean and sharp. Their individual styles may have also played a part; White was a heavier, rock-oriented drummer playing from the bottom of the kit, whereas Bruford leads with the snares. In several respects, the tracks featuring White on *Yessongs* lose out in the fidelity stakes to the *Progeny: Seven Shows from Seventy-Two* box set, which was also recorded in late 1972. In his enthusiasm, Chris Welch overlooked the sonic shortcomings in his review for *Melody Maker* in May 1973:

> There probably isn't another group in the world that could sustain such a high standard of variety and brilliance over six sides of one release, and yet leave the feeling they have a lot more music to come. *Yessongs* should prove one of the album events of the year and serve as another milestone in modern rock development.

The foldout triple LP package scores highly on presentation if not on recording details. Roger Dean provides an ornate cover design, let down by the muddy brown background. Inside and on the back cover, four paintings convey a fantasy narrative that continues from the *Fragile* sleeve. A 12-page booklet designed by Dean's brother Martyn – misspelt Martin – includes photos of each band member on stage with Rick in his familiar sequined cape and several beer bottles lined up next to his

Minimoog. Poster-size prints of Dean's artwork were very popular in the 1970s and the bedroom wall decoration of choice for Yes fans.

If memory serves me well – which it rarely does these days – *Yessongs* retailed in the UK for around £5 in 1973, roughly twice the price of a single LP. Sales were impressive, especially for a triple live album, breaching the top 20 in many countries. It entered the UK chart at number seven on 26 May and spent 13 weeks in the top 100. In the USA, *Yessongs* achieved gold status two weeks after its release.

Although no other act could match Yes for sheer output in 1973, it was a pivotal year for progressive rock in general. Milestone releases include *Tubular Bells*, Pink Floyd's *The Dark Side of the Moon*, Genesis' *Selling England by the Pound*, Emerson, Lake & Palmer's *Brain Salad Surgery*, King Crimson's *Larks' Tongues in Aspic*, Jethro Tull's *A Passion Play*, Mahavishnu Orchestra's *Birds of Fire*, Gentle Giant's *In A Glass House*, Premiata Forneria Marconi's *Photos of Ghosts*, Caravan's *For Girls Who Grow Plump in the Night*, Greenslade's *Greenslade* and *Bedside Manners are Extra*, Tangerine Dream's *Atem*, Le Orme's *Felona E Sorona*, Gong's *Flying Teapot* and *Angel's Egg*, Can's *Future Days*, Kayak's *See See the Sun*, Nektar's *Remember the Future* and *Ashes Are Burning* by Renaissance. Although not a prog album, one of the finest releases of 1973 was *Home Thoughts* by Rick Wakeman lookalike Clifford T. Ward.

Despite the competition, Yes swept the board in the 1973 *Melody Maker* annual poll, and it was a similar story in the other UK music papers. Rick was pictured at the presentation ceremony balancing a pint of beer on top of his awards. In *Sounds*, Yes were voted the top British and International band and likewise, Rick was the number one keyboard player in both categories. Chris Squire also reigned supreme and *Yessongs* was voted the number one British album, ahead of David Bowie's *Aladdin Sane* and Led Zeppelin's *Houses of the Holy*. Given this unprecedented success, a critical backlash was almost inevitable, and it would come before the year was out.

Yes – Tales from Topographic Oceans
Personnel:
Jon Anderson: lead vocals, acoustic guitar, percussion
Steve Howe: guitars, electric sitar, backing vocals
Chris Squire: bass guitar, backing vocals
Rick Wakeman: keyboards
Alan White: drums, percussion, backing vocals

Produced at Morgan Studios, London by Yes & Eddie Offord
Recording date: May – October 1973
Release date: 7 December 1973
Record label: Atlantic
Highest chart places: UK: 1, USA: 6, Canada: 4
Running time: 81:14
All tracks written by Jon Anderson, Steve Howe, Chris Squire, Rick
Wakeman, Alan White
Side one: The Revealing Science of God – Dance of the Dawn (20:27). Side
two: The Remembering – High the Memory (20:38). Side three: The Ancient
– Giants Under the Sun (18:34). Side four: Ritual – Nous Sommes du Soleil
(21:35)

Referring to *Tales from Topographic Oceans* in 2007, the *Classic Rock
Presents Prog Rock* magazine made the bold statement: '...You either
love it or hate it'. I disagree; there's a school of thought that it would
have made a very good single LP, although for your author, at just over
81 minutes, it's fine as it is.

Singer Jon Anderson had asserted himself as the band's leader and
visionary and buoyed by the success of the side-long 'Close to the Edge',
he set his sights even higher. Having composed with bassist Chris Squire
on the earlier albums, he had an ally in guitarist Steve Howe who was
equally ambitious. *The Yes Album*, *Fragile* and *Close to the Edge* had
all raised the bar, so a double concept album seemed like a natural
progression. In *Yes: The Authorised Biography* Anderson explained: 'I
wanted to try something really extravagant, in the sense that it would
take a lot of learning, a lot of preparation, and a lot of time'.

During the Japanese leg of the band's Spring tour, he immersed
himself in Paramahansa Yogananda's *Autobiography of a Yogi*, or more
specifically, the detailed footnote. The book had been recommended
to Anderson by King Crimson percussionist Jaime Muir when they met
at Bill Bruford's wedding in March. The four-part Shastric scriptures
described by Yogananda set the wheels in motion for a four-sided epic
which Anderson developed with Howe over the coming months. Vera
Stanley-Alder's writing, especially *The Finding of the Third Eye*, also had
a profound effect on Anderson's impressionistic lyrics.

With many late hours spent in hotel rooms, they put together four
distinct sections, with parts one and two virtually complete by the time
they reached Savannah, Georgia, in April. They met initial resistance

when the composition was presented to the rest of the band and while they were unsure of their parts at times, they all pitched in to make the album a success. Two months were spent at Emerson, Lake & Palmer's Manticore studios in Fulham, moulding the material into four, 20-minute sections. Although while Rick's compositional input was relatively minimal compared with the others as is his role as a soloist, his contributions as arranger and interpreter are never in doubt. His apathy towards the concept and the music, however, made it difficult to fully engage in the recording sessions. He was also preoccupied with his second solo project, which premiered just six weeks after the release of *Topographic Oceans*.

With producer Eddie Offord's backing, Anderson and Rick suggested they record in a rural location, but Howe and Squire preferred the familiar environment of a London studio. To relieve the tension, manager Brian Lane filled the studio with flora and fauna and model cows which was seized upon by the press as an example of the band's growing pretentiousness. During the sessions, Rick spent time hanging out with Black Sabbath, who were recording *Sabbath Bloody Sabbath* in the adjacent studio. Although the recording proved to be a test of endurance, Yes' dedication and the heroic work of Offord ensured the whole complex process came to a fruitful end. Sonically, it was their best-recorded album to date. When interviewed by Chris Welch for *Melody Maker* in 1973, Anderson predicted: 'People who didn't get on with *Close to the Edge* won't like this one either, unless they are prepared to sacrifice some time to get into it'.

Certainly, the hymnal, mantra-like chant that opens 'The Revealing Science of God' may have perplexed some listeners. A two-minute, ambient instrumental intro was also recorded – as incorporated in the 2003 reissue – but never made the original LP. White's snare volley and Rick's synth fanfare launches the first of three main sections where guitar and Minimoog play a jaunty tune in 6/8 with a calypso-style rhythm. The harmonised vocals are rich and fulsome, and a moment of quiet reflection features spiralling guitar, delicate bass fills and ascending Mellotron strings.

The words have a universal resonance with evolution, ecological and anti-war themes in the verses and an underlying message that young people hold the key to the future: 'Move over glory to sons of old fighters past'. An instrumental sequence follows, featuring contrasting guitar solos supported by prominent bass and drums with synth, piano and Mellotron embellishments. The electrifying Moog solo at 16:50 is one of Rick's finest, crackling with energy and the triumphant vocal melody that concludes is a throwback to the similarly grandiose finale to 'Close to the Edge'. 'The Revealing Science of God' was deservedly resurrected in later years and performed on the 2002 American tour by the reformed 1973 line-up.

In 1974, Anderson said of side two: 'We try to recall our lives and, in so doing, get the listener to recall his. It's best described as a calm sea of music'. His description is apt; 'The Remembering' combines folksy song elements with quasi-classical, instrumental interludes. It begins with a wistful Moog and electric sitar theme and in keeping with Anderson's description, there's a nautical thread that runs through the dream-like opening section. The haunting Moog and Mellotron arrangement hinted at 4:35 before blossoming at 7:35 is one of the high points of *Topographic Oceans*. One would have anticipated Rick to be responsible for writing this sequence but White claimed the credit in 1974. In the second section, a lively instrumental sequence is glued together by Squire's stunning fretless bass playing. The word 'Relayer' begins each line of the chorus and the vocal melody features lute, Mellotron flute and organ. The final section returns to the themes established earlier, only with a greater sense of urgency with an elaborate chord sequence. Moog, Mellotron, cymbal washes and weeping guitar evoke a sense of anticipation and at 18:30, the soaring guitar and keys finale from side one is reprised for the uplifting conclusion.

For many listeners, side three, 'The Ancient' proved to be the most challenging. In 1974 Anderson explained: 'It's all about the ancients: civilisations like the Incas, the Mayas and Atlantis'. True to his concept, 'The Ancient' is a mostly successful interpretation of indigenous, ethnic music, conjuring up images of abandoned temples and tropical jungles. From the rhythmic discord of a crashing gong, splashing hi-hats, vibraphone and piercing steel guitar, a melody evolves on a soft cushion of strings, and Anderson's harmonised vocals are followed by a gorgeous Moog and Mellotron theme. At 6:07, a guitar-driven groove provides the foundation for Anderson's chanted references to the 'Sun' in several languages and the Mellotron strings – with a hint of choir – are an utter delight.

At 8:24, a four-minute sequence is Yes at their most dissonant with percussion and strings contrasting with reverberated guitar. At 12:20, the mayhem subsides, and the listener's staying power is rewarded with the album's most accessible song. In a traditional verse-chorus format, 'Leaves of Green' is a eulogy to lost civilisations destroyed by foreign invaders that claimed to be acting in the name of God. Keyboard strings shimmer delightfully below Anderson's verses and the harmonised chorus. The extended classical guitar solo was later performed on stage by Howe as an alternative to the perennials 'Clap' and 'Mood for a Day'.

Wisely, Yes saved the best till last. In 1974, Anderson described 'Ritual' as 'A love song, something very personal'. Following the introduction of two new melodies with synth doubling the vocals, solo guitar recapitulates several of the album's earlier themes, incorporating a snippet of 'Close to the Edge'. It flows into the romantic song 'Nous sommes du Soleil' – 'We are of the sun' – with strings and choral backing. It builds to a majestic peak, followed by masterful solos from Squire and Howe. At 14:20, a dramatic percussive sequence represents the conflict between love and hate. It was a real showstopper when performed live with White's furious solo accompanied by Anderson on percussion and Squire hammering the kettle drums. Throughout, Roger Dean's animated drum riser spewed lights around the auditorium while Rick's shrilling synth poured on the heat. At 16:55, stately guitar heralds a moment of calm and serenity – love has triumphed. There is a sense of closure and coming to a journey's end – 'Flying home, going home'. Guitars, organ and graceful piano accompanies Anderson's yearning reprise of 'Nous Sommes du Soleil', bringing the song and the album to a moving finale. The piano part was written by White and later embellished by Rick. 'Ritual' has enjoyed the most staying power as a stage song and features on several live albums, including *Yesshows* in 1980.

The album artwork is perhaps Roger Dean's most iconic. In 2002, *Rolling Stone* readers voted it the best cover of all time, although the images suggested by Anderson and White seem out of place in the overall landscape. Back in 1973, your author mused that the five fishes on the back of the gatefold represent the band members, with one fish – clearly a different species – being Rick. I'm only speculating, of course.

Similar to the hostile reception that greeted Jethro Tull's *A Passion Play* five months earlier, the rock press poured scorn on the album and the attendant concerts. The headline by *Melody Maker* scribe Chris Welch, normally a champion of prog rock, was typical: 'Yes – Adrift on the Oceans'. *Sounds* was similarly dismissive with the headline 'Yes: Wishy Washy Tales from the Deep'. The album title gave critics ample scope to apply their watery adjectives. In his book *Close to the Edge: The Story of Yes,* published in 1999, Welch mirrored the thoughts of Yes fans back in 1973 when he admitted, 'My review of the album was surprisingly harsh'.

It's my theory that at the time, the reviewers, who had strict deadlines to meet, would have had little time to fully digest four continuous sides of often complex music. As such, the comments may have been knee-jerk reactions and only later, given more time, could they formulate an unbiased opinion. Several double LPs were released in 1973, including The Who's *Quadrophenia* and Elton John's *Goodbye Yellow Brick Road* which comprised 17 songs each and were generally well received. The bad press had the inevitable negative effect on band morale and Jon Anderson and Steve Howe went to great lengths to defend their creation. Chris Squire was more receptive to criticism as he acknowledged in *Yes: The Authorised Biography*:

Sure, the idea was logical to an extent, but the realisation of a work that size, and how big an undertaking it was, wasn't fully appreciated by everyone concerned. It missed with a lot of people because of that. I realised, even at the time, that there could have been a lot more done to make the album hold together a bit better. I wouldn't have cut it down, I just would have spent more time – but then that's my penchant, as you know.

Rick, on the other hand, was far more direct in his unwavering views:

Experimentation is fine, but it's something you should do in your own time as you're writing and rehearsing the music, until the experiment is proven in your own mind. Once you've finished experimenting, and know where things are going, then you can put the music on record.

Some 25 years later in *Close to the Edge: The Story of Yes*, Rick had a more balanced view:

I'll own up. Jon and I have had some conversations about this since. We both agree that if CDs had been available, then there was enough good material on that album to make a 50-minute CD. We had a bit too much to go on an album of 36 minutes but not enough for a double album. So it was padded mercifully. And that really upset me.

Given that *Topographic Oceans* was a product of high aspirations, the band would have been comforted by the favourable reception from the music critics in the UK daily broadsheets. *The Observer* enthused: '*Tales from Topographic Oceans*, an 80-minute, four-movement work of Wagnerian proportions. Already the piece is being applauded as a masterpiece of contemporary music'. Fans, by and large, agreed with this sentiment and responded with their feet and wallets. In the UK, it had the distinction of being the first album to achieve gold status on the strength of pre-orders alone. At the end of December, while the rest of the nation was toasting in the New Year, Yes celebrated *Topographic Oceans* reaching the top of the album chart with ELP's *Brain Salad Surgery* snapping at its heels.

Topographic Tour

Three weeks before the release of the album, the mammoth *Topographic Oceans* tour rolled into action on 16 November. It was an ambitious undertaking on every level, including duration, setlist and production values. Along with *Close to the Edge*, the new album was played in its entirety, presenting a challenge to both the audience and the attendant journalists. When the show reached London on 20 November for five consecutive sold-out shows at the Rainbow Theatre, the knives were out. It didn't help that the critics had not had the opportunity to hear and assimilate the 90 minutes of new music before the concerts. The headline for Steve Peacock's review in *Sounds* was typical: 'Yes: Close to boredom'.

For the record, your author saw three of the London shows and the Leicester De Montfort Hall performance on 26 November and like a fine wine, the new material matured with each successive performance. Roger and brother Martyn Dean were responsible for the spectacular stage design, which included a beetle-shaped canopy above the drum riser that opened out like the petals of a giant flower. A towering fibreglass structure shaped like organ pipes stood behind Rick's keyboards and a tunnel allowed the band to enter unseen onto the centre of the stage. In an era of ambitious stage productions, spearheaded by bands like ELP, Genesis and Pink Floyd, Yes set new standards.

One particular incident at Manchester's Free Trade Hall involving a takeaway curry has become part of the Rick Wakeman legend. The last date of the UK leg was in Edinburgh on 10 December, but Rick had little time for rest. He was planning a prestigious concert of his own, scheduled for the post-New Year interval prior to the resumption of the *Topographic Oceans* tour. Manager Brian Lane suggested a line-up of star names, but Rick rejected the idea on the grounds that it would distract from the music. Instead, he turned to a group of unknown musicians who were drinking buddies that he busked with at the weekends.

Prior to the tour, Rick had been finding it hard to come to terms with *Topographic Oceans* and one Sunday as a respite, he drove his Rolls Royce, registration plate RW 100, to the Valiant Trooper pub in Holmer Green, Buckinghamshire, to see an old friend. Singer Ashley Holt, along with drummer Barney James, bassist Roger Newell and Paul Randall, held regular jam sessions at the pub and Rick asked if he could join them the following Sunday. James and Newell had not previously met Rick, but the bassist was a Yes fan, so was very aware of his kudos. The Valiant Trooper became a regular Sunday night hangout for Rick and each week, he would bring more keyboards. Then one evening, out of the blue, he popped the all-important question to Holt, James, and Newell. In *Classic Rock* magazine in 2012, the latter recalled: 'He asked: 'Do you guys fancy doing a one-off gig?' That was literally all he said. We replied: 'Yeah, yeah, yeah' but nobody took any real notice'.

In Rick's recollections, he gave the trio the details of the concert as he was leaving the pub, but Newell remembers it differently. It was only later, when he read the front page of *Melody Maker* with their names mentioned, that he realised the enormity of what they had let themselves in for. Ashely Holt wryly added: 'Basically, we started panicking from that day onwards!'

1974 - Going Underground

> I was only twelve when I first read Journey to the Centre of the Earth, and I knew even then that it was always going to be the story I wanted to tell.
> Rick, quoted on the front cover of *Classic Rock Presents Rick Wakeman* in 2012.

1974 was a game-changing year for Rick. In January, he unveiled his most popular work; in March, his second child was born; in May, he made one of the most difficult decisions of his career;in July, he suffered a heart attack, and in September, he launched a global tour with an orchestra and choir. He was just 25 years of age.

With Ashely Holt, Roger Newell and Barney James on board, session guitarist Mike Egan from *The Six Wives* album returned and Gary Pickford-Hopkins from the band Wild Turkey was enlisted as co-vocalist. A&M Records had been disappointed by the absence of a singer on *The Sixth Wives,* so this time Rick was taking no chances. Three weeks of intense rehearsals followed at Rick's home in Gerrards Cross and although their new employer put the band through their paces, he was also supportive. Nonetheless, it must have seemed like a baptism of fire. Drummer Barney James revealed in 2012: 'I had never worked in such high energy time signatures before. As the rehearsals began, my hands began to look like chopped liver'.

On a tight budget, there was only limited time for the newly assembled sextet to rehearse with the orchestra and choir. Initially, the band detected an air of tension across the musical divide, but when it became apparent to the orchestra members that Rick knew his crotchets from his quavers, a mutual respect developed. Back in 1969, Deep Purple had been given a hard time by a faction of the Royal Philharmonic Orchestra when they rehearsed *Concerto for Group and Orchestra*. On 18 January, the date of the concert, rehearsals continued throughout the day until Rick declared he was satisfied.

Journey to the Centre of the Earth premiered with two back-to-back performances at London's Royal Festival Hall, a prestigious venue by the River Thames normally reserved for classical concerts. It has just 3,000 seats which Rick could have filled several times over. Each show was divided into two halves and in the first part, 'Catherine Parr', 'Catherine Howard' and 'Anne Boleyn' from *The Six Wives* were performed along with a comical turn that featured minstrel dancers and the Big Ben Banjo Band. The second half was reserved for *Journey* itself and when the full company took to the stage, it was an impressive sight.

Rick was front and centre, resplendent in his white, silver-trimmed cape, surrounded by ten keyboards and a full-size grand piano. The band was to the left, behind was the 100-piece orchestra, and at the rear, the 68-strong choir. On the right, narrator David Hemmings sat in a high back Peacock chair and above him was a cinema-size screen showing excerpts – minus the sound – from the 1959 film version of *Journey to the Centre of the Earth*. These days, concerts combining orchestral music and movie footage are a regular attraction but back in 1974, it was a revelation.

On the night of the performance, Newell recalls walking onto the stage and seeing a host of celebrities in the audience, including Steve Howe in the front row. Your author can confirm Howe's presence because I was sitting directly behind him and Chris Squire. The two empty seats next to them I presumed, were reserved for Jon Anderson and Alan White, who did not show. Howe was clearly not averse to attracting attention, he wore a blue velvet jacket with his name emblazoned across the back.

Rick Wakeman – Journey to the Centre of the Earth

Rick Wakeman: 3 Mellotrons, 2 Minimoog synthesisers, grand piano, Hammond organ, Fender Rhodes electric piano, RMI electric piano, Hohner clavinet, Honky-tonk piano
Additional personnel:
Gary Pickford-Hopkins: vocals
Ashley Holt: vocals
Mike Egan: electric guitar
Roger Newell: bass guitar
Barney James: drums
David Hemmings: narration
David Measham: conductor
Danny Beckerman: choir and orchestra arrangements
Wil Malone: choir and orchestra arrangements
London Symphony Orchestra
English Chamber Choir
Recorded live at the Royal Festival Hall, London
Produced by Rick Wakeman
Production coordination: Lou Reizner

Recording date: 18 January 1974
Release date: 3 May 1974
Record label: A&M
Highest chart places: UK: 1, USA: 3, Australia: 9
Running time: 40:07
Side one: 1. The Journey (Rick Wakeman), 2. Recollection (Wakeman)
(21:11). Side two: 1. The Battle (Wakeman), 2. The Forest (Wakeman, 'In the
Hall of the Mountain King' by Edvard Grieg) (18:57)

If *The Six Wives of Henry VIII* was an ambitious debut that hinted at
Rick's taste for theatrics, the follow-up was a major leap forward. To
realise his grand scheme, Rick involved the team responsible for the
1972 orchestral version of *Tommy,* namely Lou Reizner, arranger Wil
Malone, conductor David Measham, the London Symphony Orchestra,
and the English Chamber Choir. Given their prestigious reputation, the
LSO were a much-in-demand orchestra in the 1970s and in addition
to classical concerts, they featured on several iconic film soundtracks,
including John Williams' *Star Wars.*

Whereas *Tommy* had a proven track record, *Journey* was a far riskier
venture being a new, continuous piece of music from an artist with
only one previous album to his name. The fact that it was recorded
live also presented a challenge, not least to Rick himself. He felt
unwell before and after the concert, the stress and strain and the
enormity of the project was taking its toll. He confessed in *Yes: The
Authorised Biography*: 'For the first time in my life, I was nervous as
hell. I suddenly realised that it was all down to me. I wasn't sharing the
responsibility anymore'.

Rick had hoped to record *Journey* with an orchestra as his first solo
venture, but manager Brian Lane advised that even with the $12,500
advance from A&M Records, he lacked the funds, so he wisely opted for
a keyboard-orientated album instead. When he was eventually given the
green light, A&M were not prepared to finance the studio costs, so a live
recording was agreed upon as a compromise. It was certainly a risky,
make or break undertaking for Rick and seemingly throughout, he was
dogged by cost-cutting needs.

The advance from A&M fell short of the production costs of around
£40,000, so Rick had to re-mortgage his house and refinance his Rolls
Royce. This was supplemented by his earnings from Yes and sales of
The Six Wives album. Similarly, the revenue from the *Journey* album

would fund the ambitious tour that followed. Although he's not a gambler by nature, Rick has often described himself as a 'blackjack double upper' whereby he reinvests everything in the next project.

Journey to the Centre of the Earth was first published in French in 1864 and translated into English in 1871. Prior to discovering the book in his youth, Rick's father had taken him to a performance of Prokofiev's *Peter and the Wolf,* which had a profound effect on the young Wakeman in the way that the narration and music, using leitmotifs, told a story. Rick was an avid reader and given his talents, he too felt that he could paint pictures with music. Like *The Six Wives*, he fully immersed himself in the story, deciding which parts he would cover. Rick composed most of the music at home in Gerrards Cross, explaining in *The Caped Crusader* biography in 1978: 'I sat at the piano and frantically scribbled down the notes as fast as they appeared in my brain'.

He relocated to his farmhouse in Devon with arrangers Wil Malone and Danny Beckerman and recorded a demo using Moog, Mellotron, electric piano and clavinet to demonstrate the viability of *Journey*. Conductor David Measham was suitably impressed, but A&M insisted on a single LP, so the 60 minutes of music was reduced to 40 minutes. Even so, with Rick's formal musical training to the fore, the end result straddles the world between rock and classical with consummate ease.

For the narrator, esteemed actor Richard Harris was the original choice but was unavailable, so fellow thespian David Hemmings, who was also head of Yes' management company Hemdale, volunteered his services. A natural storyteller, he was perfect for the role with an erudite but easy-going delivery. The story involves three companions who travel from Hamburg to Iceland and descend into the crater of Snaefell. Following the route of explorer Arne Saknussemm, their adventures include encounters with subterranean sea monsters and prehistoric man. They inadvertently cause a volcanic eruption and are expelled onto the surface from Mount Stromboli – Mount Etna in Rick's version.

Although the original vinyl LP is divided into four titles, Rick conceived and performed *Journey* as one continuous piece and wrote it in order from beginning to end. It begins strongly with the memorable 'The Journey' theme performed by the orchestra and choir with strident brass, crashing percussion and Minimoog snaking in and out. 35 minutes later, Rick's grand piano leads the orchestra to a triumphant finale with a slower, stately inversion of the opening theme. The choir sings the title line, followed by three suspended stabbing chords, recalling the ending of Sibelius' *Symphony No.5*, and a sustained final chord, à la Mozart's *Symphony No. 41 Jupiter*.

The sections in between are varied, with the musical emphasis alternating between the orchestra and the band, punctuated by the narration. Hemmings establishes each scene by quoting text from the book, which is then interpreted musically. A romantic, secondary theme is introduced during 'The Journey' with strings, woodwind, tuned percussion, electric piano and Mike Egan's weeping guitar backing Gary Pickford-Hopkins' sensitive vocal. The harmonies are less successful; Pickford-Hopkins has a soft voice, not unlike Jon Anderson, whereas Ashely Holt's singing is rawer, more suited to hard rock. They could almost be singing in different keys. Rick worked hard on the lyrics and at times, they are almost too elaborate with tongue-twisting rhyming couplets like: 'Crystals of opaque quartz, studded limpid tears, forming magic chandeliers, lighting blistered galleries'.

The band really come into their own at the 12:40 mark, where cascading strings herald a funky instrumental section with wah-wah guitar and Rick's funky Hohner clavinet channelling Stevie Wonder. Egan's playing is inspired and partly improvised, reaching a feverish pitch that borders on Steve Howe territory. Call and response exchanges between the brass instruments bring 'Recollection' to a memorable close, let down only by the off-key trumpet at 19:46.

On side two of the vinyl album, the band rock hard during 'The Battle' to represent the confrontation between the sea monsters and the storm that follows. Clavinet and Minimoog are once again to the fore, backed by Barney James' propulsive drumming and Roger Newell's throbbing bass line. Holt delivers the lines 'Save me' and 'Praise God' with suitable gusto, supported by the choir, who are excellent throughout. Their combined voices are especially effective when they are ebbing and flowing to simulate the rolling of the sea. As we head towards the home straight, the familiar strains of Grieg's 'In the Hall of the Mountain King' provide a moment of light relief, with Rick's Minimoog racing the orchestra towards the finish line.

Plans to record both the 6.00 pm and 8.00 pm performances were stymied when the orchestra demanded double pay. As a result, only the second performance was recorded using Ronnie Lane's Lynn Mobile Studio. The theory was the first show would act as a dress rehearsal and any glitches could be ironed out before the second. A week later, the sixteen-track master tape was painstakingly mixed by Rick and engineer Paul Tregurtha at London's Morgan Studios over a two-week period. They discovered flaws in the performance and timing differences between the band and the orchestra, which were glossed over with judicial editing. Some of the vocals were re-recorded due to an accident with the microphone leads during the performance.

It was Rick's intention to have the record in the shops while the concert was still fresh in people's minds, but he hit a major snag. On hearing the album, the London office of A&M were reluctant to release it, believing it would not sell. With Rick's reputation and a great deal of his money at stake, Brian Lane sent a cassette copy to Jerry Moss, the head of A&M in California. Fortunately, he liked what he heard and overruled the London office. His faith in Rick paid off; on 25 May, it was the label's first number one album in the UK and spent 30 weeks in the chart. In America, it lingered in the *Billboard* 200 chart for 27 weeks and worldwide, went on to sell more than 15 million copies.

Journey was nominated for both an Ivor Novello Award and a Grammy in America and although some critics found Rick's classical pretensions hard to swallow, most remained open-minded. Steve Peacock's review of the concert in *Sounds* was patronising and complimentary in equal measures:

> The temptation to write a work based on obscure religious teachings by a sixteenth-century Peruvian sage, or to set *War and Peace* to music must be strong for a man in Rick Wakeman's position – one imagines that would be the kind of thing to send his Yes audience into paroxysms of self-congratulatory delight. But happily, he took Jules Verne's spectacular yarn, and made a straightforward spectacular production number out of it.

Unwittingly, the comment regarding *War and Peace* would prove to be prophetic before the year was out. Chris Welch's album review in *Melody Maker* was refreshingly perceptive:

> From the open shout of the orchestra, the rumble of tympani and the delicate ringing of the vibraphone, the mood is set for romance and adventure. In classical music terms, the composition might be described as 'lightweight' or of 'little consequence'. But as far as popular music is concerned, Rick's composition for choir, orchestra and group is entertaining, fresh and disarmingly unpretentious. There are no

attempts to be arty, clever or super-technical. This could be a score for a Hollywood musical – tuneful, but with epic overtones.

The original LP sleeve evokes the underground world of Verne's story, laced with elements of humour. The cover features a hazy photo of the band, orchestra, and choir on stage where curiously, Rick's hair has been conspicuously painted over to look more blond. The ten-page gatefold features a surreal montage of images, including two lizards swimming in foaming pints of beer, a sly reference to the fake dinosaurs in the 1959 film version. The band is listed simply as 'The Band' – the English Rock Ensemble moniker would come later.

Journey has proven to be Rick's most enduring work, with or without vocals. A fine 45-minute instrumental arrangement was performed during the *Wakeman with Wakeman* shows with his son Adam in the early 1990s. Rick released *Return to the Centre of the Earth* in 1999, but despite the presence of star guest singers, almost inevitably, it's overshadowed by its predecessor. The 2012 extended re-recording of *Journey,* on the other hand, arguably improves on the original, especially the impeccable orchestrations and previously unreleased songs performed by Hayley Sanderson. At almost 60 minutes, it's how Rick originally envisaged the work. Fittingly, in July 2019, Rick returned to the Royal Festival Hall for two performances of *Journey*, complete with narrator, orchestra and choir, to celebrate his 70th birthday.

With both Rick and Yes enjoying number one albums in 1974, other UK chart-topping successes that year include *Band on the Run* by Paul McCartney & Wings, *Diamond Dogs* by David Bowie, *Caribou* by Elton John, *Elton John's Greatest Hits, Hergest Ridge* by Mike Oldfield, *The Singles: 1969 –1973* by The Carpenters, *Smiler* by Rod Stewart, *Old New Borrowed and Blue* by Slade, and let's not forget *Rollin'* by the Bay City Rollers. In the USA, the list includes two albums by John Denver, *Planet Waves* by Bob Dylan, *Chicago VII, 461 Ocean Boulevard* by Eric Clapton, *Fulfillingness' First Finale* by Stevie Wonder, *Walls and Bridges* by John Lennon, *It's Only Rock 'n' Roll* by the Rolling Stones, and the wryly titled *Not Fragile* by Bachman-Turner Overdrive.

Time to Say Goodbye

The second leg of Yes' *Tales from Topographic Oceans* tour got underway in North America on 7 February. Despite the enthusiastic reception from the fans, Rick had been disenchanted by the concerts during the UK leg the previous year and the taste of solo success with *Journey* added fuel to his discontent. The set structure remained the same, with the three songs from *Close to the Edge* performed in reverse order and the second part dedicated to the latest album. Gradually, however, Yes replaced the newer material with proven stage favourites like 'Starship Trooper'. 'The Remembering' was the first casualty and when it was dropped from the setlist at the end of February, it would never return.

It wasn't all bad vibes, however. Following a performance in February at New York's Madison Square Garden – a popular stronghold for Yes in America – Rick enthusiastically informed biographer Dan Wooding: 'We played well tonight. It was the kind of show I wish we could play every night. The best Yes concert I've ever experienced'. Having missed the birth of Oliver in 1972 while touring America with Yes, Rick was 4,600 miles from home in Oklahoma City when his second son Adam was born on 11 March 1974. In the November 2003 edition of *Billboard* magazine celebrating Yes' 35th Anniversary, Rick reflected on the period:

> The low points to me were certainly around the *Topographic Oceans* era. I couldn't get into the direction the music was going, and Yes is always a give-and-take. Having to make the decision to leave, that was a low point. If you can't get into the music, you have to ethically say 'Hold on, I can't help the band here, it's time to move on'.

Following a two-week pause, the tour continued in mainland Europe on 11 April. The first port of call was Frankfurt, where Rick called a band meeting and tried to hand in his notice. The others persuaded him to continue and to delay his decision until after the tour. He reluctantly agreed. Following the last date in Rome on 23 April, he reiterated his decision to leave, although he felt the band wasn't taking him seriously. Rick retreated with his family to his farmhouse in Devon, where free from distractions, he could think things through. He has told the story of what happened next many times, including this version in the *Say Yes!* autobiography:

> May 18th 1974, was a day I will never forget for as long as I live. It started with a mid-morning phone call from Brian Lane, telling me that rehearsals for the new Yes album would be starting the following week. I told him I would not be there. Five minutes after I put the

phone down it rang again. This time it was Terry O'Neil from A&M Records. 'Rick, I've got sensational news for you. *Journey to the Centre of the Earth* has just gone to number one in the UK album charts'. May 18th 1974, was my 25th birthday.

It's a good story, even though on the date in question, *Journey* entered the official UK chart at 14, reaching number one on 25 May. Exactly two weeks later, Rick was once again pictured on the front page of the UK music weeklies. *Melody Maker* ran the headline 'Rick Wakeman Quits Yes' while *New Musical Express* went with a more succinct 'Wakeman Quits Yes'.

According to the other band members, there was always an uncertainty regarding Rick's leaving until it actually happened. Undaunted, a four-piece Yes put together new material for what would become *Relayer* before tackling the difficult task of finding a replacement. Vangelis Papathanassiou was Anderson's first choice, but his gregarious talent and personality proved to be too overpowering to be confined within a band environment. Around eight keyboardists were auditioned over a six-week period and in 1980, Jon Anderson recalled: 'We just couldn't seem to find the man who could replace Rick. Someone who had a similar talent. A wide keyboard spectrum. We still wanted that colour'.

Then in August, Patrick Moraz from the trio Refugee – essentially The Nice mark two – entered the picture. Like Rick, Moraz was a virtuoso keyboardist who had studied piano from the age of five. A native of Switzerland, he also has the distinction of being the first foreigner to join the ranks of Yes, although he would not be the last. As of the time of writing – September 2022 – the band's American touring members outnumber the English contingent by three to two.

Coincidentally, one of the keyboardists on Yes' shortlist was Nick Glennie-Smith. In 1974, he joined the band Wally who were managed by Brian Lane and prior to his arrival, Rick, together with *The Old Grey Whistle Test* presenter Bob Harris produced the band's self-titled debut album.

Rick's first full-blown stage presentation of *Journey* following the album release was at London's Crystal Palace Bowl on Saturday, 27 July, where Yes had played in September 1972. The support acts included Procol Harum, Leo Sayer, Gryphon, and Wally. It was an ambitious affair and during 'The Battle' sequence, two large inflatable dinosaurs squared off in the shallow lake in front of the stage. As was the case with many of Rick's ventures at the time, 'grandiosity' was the byword. The show began as it had done at the Royal Festival Hall with material from *The Six Wives* performed by Rick and his five-piece band before being joined on a cramped stage by the New World Symphony Orchestra, the English Chamber Choir and David Hemmings once again providing the narration from the wicker chair. Following the payment issue in January, Rick vetoed the London Symphony Orchestra, although he relented in 1998 for the recording of *Return to the Centre of the Earth*.

Unbeknown to the audience and most of those on stage, Rick had been unwell before the show due to the enormous pressure he was under. He was also drinking and smoking heavily and was rarely in bed before four am. Thanks to some liquid refreshment before the performance, outwardly, he appeared calm and relaxed. The following day, however, he suffered a heart attack and was rushed into Wexham Park Hospital in Slough, Berkshire. He spent several weeks there recuperating, and to pass the time, he began writing his next magnum-opus *The Myths and Legends of King Arthur,* with furtive use of a portable cassette recorder. Rick later described the album as autobiographical, given that it could have easily been his last.

Undaunted, he ignored the advice of specialists and, in September, embarked on a month-long trek around North America. His six-man band had become a full-time unit comprising Gary Pickford-Hopkins and Ashley Holt vocals, Roger Newell bass, Barney James drums, Jeffrey Crampton guitars and John Hodgson percussion. Although Rick had racked up the air miles with Yes, it was his first trip across the Atlantic under his own name. David Hemmings was unavailable, so Shakespearean actor Terry Taplin came along as narrator, with David Measham once again waving the baton. In New York, the 45-strong National Philharmonic Orchestra and 16-voiced Choir of America were assembled specifically for the tour. In *The Caped Crusader* biography, Rick explained:

> When I first arrived in New York and began rehearsals with the orchestra, I could see they thought I was joking; just a long-haired nutter. After all, what was a young upstart like me doing hiring them and taking them across the States? But after a few days, we all began to loosen up and they began to enjoy my music.

To minimise expenditure, they played 22 venues in just 25 days. Even so, the cost of hiring and transporting the entire entourage in a

Lockheed Electra private airliner plus expenses set Rick back $243,000. Rick's philosophy was, do not to short-change your audience and the theory was that the outlay on touring would be justified by increased record sales.

Like the Royal Festival Hall and Crystal Palace performances, the set showcased *The Sixth Wives, Journey* in its entirety plus 'Concerto for American Commercial Television', which adds a Copland-esque grandeur to TV tunes like *The Flintstones*. One of the shows recorded 'Live somewhere in Canada' was captured in part for the *Unleashing the Tethered One* bootleg, released on vinyl in 1974 and on CD twenty years later. According to the *Yes Music Circle* fanzine magazine in February 1993, Rick considers this performance of *Journey* superior to the original album version. The band and orchestra certainly sound tight and well-rehearsed.

Financial implications aside, the tour was a huge success, concluding in October with two sold-out shows at New York's Madison Square Garden. Back in the UK, Rick had again been voted 'Top International keyboard player' in the *Melody Maker* reader's poll, but he wasn't about to let complacency set in and immediately began work on his next album.

As he had done for *The Six Wives*, Rick meticulously researched *The Myths and Legends of King Arthur and the Knights of the Round Table*, reading eight of the numerous books on the subject. He found many conflicting accounts – not unlike your author's experience when researching Rick's career for this book– before settling on six of the most colourful stories. Rick explained his initial fascination with the legend to author Dan Wooding:

There is a little village called Trevalga, which is about six miles from Tintagel, the site where some believe was Arthur's castle. When I was five years old, I stayed down there on a farm for five months and spent a lot of time in Tintagel. It stuck in my mind from then.

Again, there was no expense spared. The album boasts his six-man band, narrator Terry Taplin, the 44-strong English Chamber Choir led by Guy Protheroe, the eight-voiced Nottingham Festival Vocal Group and the 47-piece New World Orchestra assembled by orchestral contractor David Katz. Following two-and-half weeks of rehearsals, the album was recorded at London's Morgan Studios over a twelve-week period

– interrupted by the Christmas and New Year holidays. His regular engineer, however, had initial reservations, as Rick explained:

When I first started planning it, I told Paul Tregurtha what I wanted to do, and he told me that it was technically impossible. There were just not enough tracks on the recording machine to produce the final required mix.

As a footnote to the year, Yes' *Relayer* album was released at the end of November and Rick was invited onto the BBC Radio One Saturday afternoon rock show to voice his opinion. He acknowledged that 'Soon' was one of the most beautiful songs Yes had recorded, but otherwise, he felt that the album was evidence that he had made the right decision in leaving the band six months earlier.

1975 – Myths, Magic, and a Nineteenth-Century Keyboard Star

It's a funny feeling being on stage. I really can't describe it. If it's right, it's the closest thing to heaven, a kind of factual dream, the ultimate in happiness. When it goes wrong, it's a natural low.
Rick Wakeman quoted in *The Caped Crusader* biography.

As 1975 rolled around, Rick's flair for showmanship was at its peak. He had amassed £85,000 worth of instruments and two-14-metre-long articulated trucks were required to transport seventeen tons of equipment – enough to fill the cargo hold of a 747. His hands were his most valuable asset, however, which he insured for one million dollars. On tour, there was always plenty of humour between the band members on and off stage, but Rick remained deadly serious about his work. Due to his warm-hearted nature, he was known to friends and family as 'Uncle Rick'.

In January, with *King Arthur* barely in the can, Rick hit the road once more. *Journey to the Centre of the Earth* had been a global success and by way of appreciation, he headed east to Japan, Australia, and New Zealand, where he had built a considerable fanbase. A live recording on 4 February at the Sydney Mayer Music Bowl in Melbourne was released on video in 1993 and later DVD/CD. Featuring the Melbourne Philharmonic Orchestra and Chamber Choir in front of a 30,000 strong Aussie crowd, it's a rare example of a large-scale production from this era on film. Two weeks earlier, a concert at the Koseinenkin Hall in Osaka, Japan, on 21 January was recorded and later released as the two-CD bootleg *Journeyman.*

The setlist for the tour included 'Guinevere' and 'Merlin the Magician' from the yet-to-be-released *King Arthur*; otherwise, there were few changes from the Royal Festival Hall performance twelve months earlier. When Rick returned to the UK in March, the new studio album was unveiled, and expectations were high.

Rick Wakeman – The Myths and Legends of King Arthur and the Knights of the Round Table
Personnel:
Rick Wakeman: synthesisers, keyboards, grand piano
Gary Pickford-Hopkins: lead vocals

Ashley Holt: lead vocals
Jeffrey Crampton: lead and acoustic guitars
Roger Newell: bass guitar
Barney James: drums
John Hodgson: percussion
Terry Taplin: narrator
Guy Protheroe: choirmaster
David Measham: choir and orchestra conductor
David Katz: orchestral coordination
Wil Malone: orchestral arrangements
New World Orchestra
English Chamber Choir
Nottingham Festival Vocal Group
Produced at Morgan Studios, London by Rick Wakeman
Recording date: 16 October 1974 – 10 January 1975
Release date: 27 March 1975
Record label: A&M
Highest chart places: UK: 2, USA: 21, Australia: 2
Running time: 44:57
All songs and music written by Rick Wakeman
Side one: 1. Arthur (7:26), 2. Lady of the Lake (0:45), 3. Guinevere (6:45), 4. Sir Lancelot and the Black Knight (5:21). Side two: 1. Merlin the Magician (8:51), 2. Sir Galahad (5:51), 3. The Last Battle (9:41)

King Arthur is one of the most popular characters in English literature and his exploits have attracted many writers and filmmakers. Not surprisingly, Rick was the first to devote a concept album to the subject – the musical *Camelot* notwithstanding. If his first album was based on sixteenth-century English royalty and his second, a nineteenth-century fantasy novel, his third delves even deeper into the past and the folklore surrounding this sixth-century British king. In addition to satisfying Rick's passion for heritage and pageantry, *King Arthur* completed a three-album cycle that embraced the grandiose and a desire to tell stories with music and songs. His piano teacher Dorothy Symes had encouraged him to formulate pictures in his head when listening to and playing music, and Rick's compositions were a reversal of that process. While his concepts are on a grand scale, the subjects are part of popular culture, designed to appeal to a mass audience, unlike the often ambiguous, spiritual quests presented by Jon Anderson and Yes.

In terms of narrative, the book that Rick's album most closely resembles is *King Arthur and His Knights of the Round Table*. First published in 1953. Intended for children, it's one of the most entertaining – if not factual – accounts of the Arthurian legends. Rick explained the concept to author Dan Wooding:

Most of the album is centred around swords because there are three famous swords which feature throughout the legends. There is Excalibur, which is the sword that came from the Lady of the Lake. There is the sword which was first pulled out of an anvil in the churchyard. The story was that whoever pulled the sword out would become King of England. And Arthur pulled it out. ...And the other sword story is the one with Sir Galahad, which is a sword which was floating down the river.

Rick's evocative music for *King Arthur* recalls classic film composers like Erich Wolfgang Korngold and Miklós Rózsa, noted for their lavish scores for historical dramas. The main 'Arthur' theme oozes chivalry and heraldry, although, in the UK, it will always be associated with politics thanks to the BBC adopting it for their coverage of government elections. Following Terry Taplin's solemn introduction, the brassy opening gives way to Rick's stately Minimoog melody, with Gary Pickford-Hopkins and Ashley Holt once again sharing vocal honours and the choir bringing up the rear. Arthur has pulled the sword from the anvil to earn his place on the throne.

The 'Lady of the Lake' is sung in the first person by the all-male Nottingham Festival Vocal Group and not, as you might expect, the female members of the choir. 'Guinevere' opens with a courtly, acoustic piano solo, signifying that as the queen, her rightful place is by Arthur's side. But she loves Lancelot, as represented by the romantic ballad that follows, backed by high strings, piano, and synth. The mood is broken by Rick's sizzling Moog solo and Jeffrey Crampton's bluesy guitar break.

'Sir Lancelot and the Black Knight' is the album's most powerful song and opens with another muscular orchestral theme. Holt is in his heavy rock element and the choir spurs on the two opposing knights with the aggressive 'Fight' hook. The impossibly fast instrumental punctuations keep the orchestra on their toes and Barney James and Roger Newell lay down a lively samba rhythm for Rick's searing solo featuring weaving synth lines .

Side two opens with 'Merlin the Magician', the album's most enduring track. It goes through several changes to emphasise the eccentric nature of Merlin's character. The Nottingham Festival Vocal Group returns for the solemn introduction, followed by piano and harpsichord to set the scene. Three very different instrumental sections are juxtaposed, beginning with a lovely piano theme. A prominent bass line provides the springboard for Minimoog soloing and the manic, honky tonk piano and orchestra sequence is pure Keystone Cops. 'Merlin' became a live staple and during the 1990s, Rick added lyrics to represent how he'd originally envisaged the piece.

'Sir Galahad' reprises several motifs from the previous tracks, including the choral and piano introduction from 'Merlin' and the orchestral theme from 'Sir Lancelot and the Black Knight'. The song part is original, however, an organ-led romp with a calypso shuffle rhythm where Holt's strident verses contrast with Pickford-Hopkins' mellow middle-eight. Galahad, son of Sir Lancelot, is encouraged by Arthur to pull a sword of his own from a stone, although the young knight gives his prize to Sir Gawain.

The final track is one of the first pieces Rick wrote for *King Arthur* while convalescing in hospital the previous August. 'The Last Battle' mourns the passing of the Knights of the Round Table and the fall of Britain to the invading Saxons. Arthur confronts the treacherous Mordred and they mortally wound each other. It's a suitably stirring finale, reprising the 'Arthur' theme and there's even a rippling piano nod to 'Catherine Howard' at the 4:46 mark. Terry Taplin intones a poignant epitaph and with a final flourish from the orchestra and choir, the reign of King Arthur comes to an end.

The LP gatefold sleeve is suitably classy, with Rick's name and the title presented as a royal seal. A richly illustrated twelve-page booklet includes the lyrics and the names of every member of the orchestra and choir. A note for trivia fans; apart from the film soundtracks *Lisztomania* and *White Rock*, *King Arthur* is Rick's only album sleeve of the 1970s where he's not pictured on the cover.

Like its predecessor, *King Arthur* was an unqualified success and Rick's third gold album in a row. It breached the top five in many countries, including Japan, Australia, and New Zealand, where the recent tour had paid dividends. Healthy sales in Brazil encouraged Rick to perform there later in the year. It spent 28 weeks in the UK chart and on 19 April, only the immovable *The Best of the Stylistics* kept it off the top spot. It went on to sell over twelve million copies worldwide and like the subject, it became a legend – in Rick's musical catalogue, at least. Understandably, 'period' themed albums was a style he would return to in later years. *King Arthur* was equally well received by the critics and Dom Lawson in *Classic Rock* magazine later enthused:

> What really takes the breath away about this album nearly 40 years on from its release is how exuberant and brimming with energy it is. From the mysterious, sombre drift of the opening 'Arthur' onwards, these are songs that strike an enchanting balance between complexity and melodic heft, as surging Mellotrons and squelching Moogs collide with real choirs, vivacious orchestral interventions and the exhilarating thrum and thump of live guitars, bass and drums.

Coincidentally, the release of *King Arthur* was followed a week later by the film *Monty Python and the Holy Grail* which took a satirical sideswipe at the same subject. Although silly characters like 'Brave Sir Robin' and the 'Knights Who Say Ni!' are absent from Rick's concept, the album and the film proved to be popular with the same age demographic.

Just as *Journey to the Centre of the Earth* received a makeover in 2012, Rick recorded and released an extended version of *King Arthur* in 2016. A double CD, it features no less than thirteen additional tracks – 40 minutes of additional music – with new artwork courtesy of Roger Dean.

King Arthur On the Rocks

Rick had planned to stage *King Arthur* near Tintagel Castle on the north coast of Cornwall, which has a long association with Arthurian legend. Although publicity photos were taken close to the site with Rick dressed as Merlin, plans were scuppered by the local authority, so he opted for somewhere closer to home. Rick set his sights on London's Wembley Stadium, but that was deemed impractical, so he turned his attention to the adjacent Empire Pool – later renamed Wembley Arena. In March 2022, he explained to Nick Krewen of the *Toronto Star*:

> When I told the management I wanted to do King Arthur on ice they laughed at me. But I persevered and did it and, after it was sort of successful, they said, 'Yeah, we thought it was a great idea from the beginning', and I thought 'you naughty little toerags'.

Although the three shows that Rick performed on ice at the Empire Pool on Friday, 30 May to Sunday, 1 June have gone down in history as his grand folly, for the 27,000 fans who paid an average ticket price of £2.50, they were a triumph. Rick had played material from *King Arthur* during the previous tour, but it was at Wembley where it was performed in its entirety for the first time.

Rick hadn't pre-planned to stage the concerts on ice, but as the rink was in place for the *Ice Follies* shows, it provided a unique opportunity to attempt something never before by a rock act. Knowing that A&M Records would not fund such an audacious project, he bankrolled the shows, which were promoted by Harvey Goldsmith, with his own money. In *Classic Rock* magazine in 2012, Rick recalled:

My accountant thought I was completely mad, and the management did shake their heads on more than one occasion. But there were so many exciting possibilities back then and I grabbed them with both hands. I wasn't being told what to do by record companies and management at the time. You had freedom to do what you wanted – and so I did.

Rick and his six-man band were joined by a 58-piece orchestra, the 48-strong English Chamber Choir, narrator Terry Taplin and to complete the entourage, around 20 professional ice skaters and a stage crew. He also imported a specialised PA system from America to ensure that every instrument was clearly audible. Bassist Roger Newell brandished a hefty custom triple-neck guitar which had been devised by Rick. The innovative instrument incorporated a six-string guitar, a four-string bass, and a fretless bass, designed and built by Wal, a friend of Newell. To capture the flavour of *King Arthur*, Rick wore a long sleeve tunic fashioned to look like chainmail under his cape. Although all three shows were a sell-out, Rick failed to recoup his costs. He had no regrets, however, even though he was reputed to be out of pocket to the tune of £38,000.

In the meantime, Rick's old band, Strawbs were still going strong even though they were without a full-time keyboard player. On the advice of their management, Strawbs parted company with A&M Records in 1975, which Dave Cousins would later regret. Recorded in the summer, *Nomadness* was their tenth and final album for the label and Cousins invited Rick to play electric harpsichord on the song 'Tokyo Rosie'. In his autobiography, Cousins recalls:

Before the session, Rick had been in the nearest pub for a couple of hours with Alan Yentob, the BBC's head of arts programming, discussing a Wakeman documentary, and when he eventually turned up to play, he was three parts to the wind. Rick fumbled around 'Tokyo Rosie' for half an hour, getting nowhere, when he suggested turning the studio lights off. We switched the lights on, and there was Rick, bollock naked, playing his socks off, although he didn't have any on.

Rick returned to the studio the next day to complete the recording and it would be his final appearance on a Strawbs album for nearly 40 years. When *Nomadness* was released in November, it failed to chart in the UK, but it did reach number 147 in the *Billboard* top 200.

Strawbs began their North American tour at the Forum in Montreal at the beginning of October and Rick appeared at the same venue the following week. Canada, and the Montreal area, in particular, was a haven for progressive rock in the 1970s, as was the east coast of the USA, especially New York and Philadelphia.

The BBC documentary referred to by Cousins was shown on 3 September in the *Success Story* television series. It focused on the highs and lows of Rick's career and included scenes at home with his family. A week later, the BBC screened a 50-minute film of the *King Arthur* on ice show at Wembley.

Rick had planned to follow *King Arthur* with another mythological epic, *A Suite of Gods*, but costs prevented an extravaganza on the scale of the two previous albums. *A Suite of Gods* did eventually appear twelve years later, but not as Rick originally intended. In the interim, there was another quite different project that he had been working on between other commitments throughout most of 1975.

Rick Wakeman - Lisztomania

Personnel:
Rick Wakeman: keyboards
David Wilde: Liszt piano music
Roger Daltrey: vocals on 'Love's Dream', 'Orpheus Song', 'Funerailles', 'Peace at Last'
Linda Lewis: vocals on 'Hell'
Paul Nicholas: vocals on 'Excelsior Song'
The English Rock Ensemble

National Philharmonic Orchestra
George Michie
John Forsythe
Produced at Island Mobile Studios and RAK Studios, London, by Rick
Wakeman
Recording date: 1975
Release date: November 1975
Record label: A&M
Highest chart places: UK: Did not chart, USA: 145, Australia: 85
Running time: 32:20
Side one: 1. Rienzi / Chopsticks Fantasia (4:20) (Richard Wagner, Franz
Liszt), 2. Love's Dream (4:25) (Liszt, Roger Daltrey), 3. Dante Period (2:05)
(Liszt), 4. Orpheus Song (3:10) (Liszt, Daltrey, Jonathan Benson), 5. Hell (1:59)
(Liszt, translation by John Forsythe). Side two: 1. Hibernation (1:11) (Rick
Wakeman), 2. Excelsior Song (2:32) (Liszt, Wakeman, Ken Russell), 3. Master
Race (0:45) (Wagner), 4. Rape, Pillage & Clap (3:09) (Wagner), 5. Funerailles
(3:48) (Liszt, Benson), 6. Free Song (Hungarian Rhapsody) (1:57) (Liszt), 7.
Peace at Last (2:59) (Liszt, Benson, Daltrey)

In February 2013, *The Guardian* news website posed the rhetorical
question: '*Lisztomania*: the most embarrassing historical film ever
made?' Written and directed by controversial filmmaker Ken Russell,
Lisztomania is a biographical musical which takes numerous liberties
with the life and music of Franz Liszt. It followed hot on the heels of
Tommy, where Russell's penchant for excess was kept mostly in check
by The Who's song cycle, which drove the narrative. With *Lisztomania*,
his imagination ran wild, resulting in an episodic, sometimes grotesque,
often farcical re-tellingly of the adulation, loves, death and reincarnation
of the nineteenth-century Hungarian composer and virtuoso ivory tickler.
   Russell signed a contract with David Puttnam's production company
Goodtimes Enterprises, to make the film and as the investor, Puttnam
had a good deal of control over the production and casting. Roger
Daltrey and Paul Nicholas – who had both appeared in *Tommy* – star
as Liszt and Richard Wagner, respectively, and Ringo Starr plays the
Pope, complete with a Liverpudlian accent. As filming progressed, the
production budget spiralled to 1.2 million.
   Rick was initially brought on board at the suggestion of Daltrey's
manager Bill Curbishley to arrange one of Liszt's piano pieces as a song
and he was asked by Russell to score the film. In addition to rearranging

compositions by Liszt and Wagner for electronic keyboards, Rick provided original music rehearsed and recorded with his band at Shepperton Studios. Arguments followed regarding which pieces would be included on the soundtrack before, eventually, a disillusioned Rick handed over the master tapes and walked out. Derek Green, head of A&M Records in the UK, confiscated the tapes until the dispute was settled. Eventually, the film company was given a free hand in making the track selections and in the process, much of Rick's input fell by the wayside.

Despite the album sleeve proclaiming 'Music produced and arranged by Rick Wakeman' on the cover and 'All selections arranged & adapted by Rick Wakeman' on the back, this was disputed by Rick. Speaking to author Dan Wooding in 1977, he was frank in his assessment of the finished product:

I thought it was dreadful, truly awful. It was nothing to do with me. There was hardly anything of mine on it in the end. I only played on a few minutes of it. I thought it was appalling mixed and dreadfully produced. They stuck my name on it as producer, but I never produced it.

It's not hard to imagine that Rick would have relished playing the lead role himself. Liszt was a piano-playing star in the 1800s, complete – in Russell's interpretation at least – with screaming girls in the audience. Instead, Rick has a cameo part as a Teutonic Frankenstein-like monster created by Wagner, who's portrayed as a neurotic fascist by Nicholas. In this bizarre piece of casting, Rick is dressed as Thor, the Norse god of thunder, with his face and hair sprayed silver. In 1984, he had a more conventional role as a photographer in Russell's fantasy thriller *Crimes and Passion*. He also provided the soundtrack, which proved to be a more fruitful experience than *Lisztomania*. In 2002, after recovering the master tapes, Rick released *The Real Lisztomania,* which was closer to his original conception.

The troubled gestation of *Lisztomania* is obvious in the finished album, although despite Rick's disconnect, there's much to savour. This is particularly true of side two, where his stately trumpet-like fanfare during 'Hibernation' raises the curtain. Two Wagner compositions retitled 'Master Race' and 'Rape, Pillage & Clap', boast rich, brassy keyboard orchestrations in the style of the late, great Vangelis, while 'Free Song' is a light-hearted, souped-up version of 'Hungarian Rhapsody

No. 13'. The latter was performed on the *No Earthly Connection* tour in 1976 and really put the English Rock Ensemble through their paces.

Elsewhere on the album, concert pianist David Wilde faithfully recreates Liszt's piano pieces. This is particularly true of the opening 'Rienzi / Chopsticks Fantasia', which takes its cue from the film with a backdrop of screaming girls, Beatlemania style. For *The Real Lisztomania*, Rick re-recorded all the piano parts in his customary florid style.

Roger Daltrey is in fine vocal form throughout, remaining true to the spirit of Liszt's tunes. 'Love's Dream' is based on 'Nocturne No. 3 Liebestraum' while 'Orpheus Song' is an adaptation of the symphonic poems 'Orpheus' and 'Heroide Funebre'. During 'Funerailles', The Who singer is supported by Wilde's strident piano hammering and the National Philharmonic Orchestra in full-on symphonic mode. 'Love's Dream' is reprised for the closing song 'Peace at Last' with strong support from Rick's funky electric piano and the band. For the 2002 rerecording, he adds a lively Moog solo to close.

Rounding out the album is a bizarre trio of tracks. Rick enters all synths blazing during 'Dante Period', turning Liszt's tune upside down in this strident evocation of his sexual escapades. The aptly titled 'Hell' closes side one where Linda Lewis' manic singing veers from punk to opera while Rick's screaming keys go into overdrive. Paul Nicholas also gives a grandstanding vocal performance during 'Excelsior Song', making the most of Russell's tongue-in-cheek salute to the master race while Rick lurches around the screen in his platform boots as Thor.

The LP sleeve is modest, with no gatefold and no lyric sheet or booklet. Daltrey features on the front cover behind a phallic symbol in the form of a raised hand holding a fencing foil. On the back cover, there are stills from the film, including Rick in his *Marvel Comics*-inspired costume. For the first time on an album sleeve, Rick's band is credited as The English Rock Ensemble, a name suggested by manager Brian Lane.

The film opened in October 1975 and the album followed a month later. They both polarised critics, although *Melody Maker* reviewer Chris Welch was generally positive:

> Russell and Wakeman seem an odd creative partnership and one that will be exposed to heavy abuse, but amidst all the bad taste and sensationalism, they produce something brutal and honest.

The film bombed at the box office and album sales suffered as a result. *Lisztomania* was Rick's only release of the 1970s not to trouble the UK charts and peaked at 145 in the *Billboard* 200. He went on to score several films over subsequent years and would have liked to have done more. Soundtracks were an obvious outlet for Rick's talents, but as he acknowledged in *Classic Rock* magazine in 2012: 'It's always difficult to produce soundtrack albums, as you're trying to please so many people and it's never possible really'.

The failure of *Lisztomania* is understandable. The cinema-going public in 1975 had a surfeit of quality films to choose from, including *Jaws, One Flew Over the Cuckoo's Nest, Dog Day Afternoon, Nashville, The Man Who Would be King, The Eiger Sanction, Sholay, The Rocky Horror Picture Show, French Connection II, Barry Lyndon, The Return of the Pink Panther,* and *Rollerball.* Yes had been approached to score the latter film, which they turned down, so classical pieces were used instead.

King Arthur Hits the Road

Before embarking on the *King Arthur* tour, there was a band reshuffle. Singer Gary Pickford-Hopkins departed, as did guitarist Jeffrey Crampton who was replaced by John Dunsterville, recommended by Roger Newell. Left-handed drummer Tony Fernandez also made his debut, replacing Barney James, and he continues to work with Rick to this day. In the absence of an orchestra, Rick bolstered the sound with the addition of Martyn Shields on trumpet and Reg Brooks on trombone. Ashley Holt, John Hodgson, and Newell remained on vocals, percussion, and bass, respectively, to complete the line-up.

The North American leg began on 7 October at New York's Madison Square Garden. They crisscrossed the Canadian border several times before finishing in early December. On several dates, they were supported by UK prog rock maestros Gentle Giant, whose star shone brighter in America than it did in their home country. Like Rick, multi-instrumentalist Kerry Minnear performed with multiple, stacked keyboards.

A show at the Winterland Ballroom in San Francisco on 2 November was recorded for American radio and released on CD in 1995 as *King Biscuit Flower Hour Presents Rick Wakeman In Concert.* The brass section, along with Rick's orchestral keys, do a fine job of reimagining an abridged *Journey.* Rick plays fast and loose with some of his original arrangements, including an extended 'Catherine Howard', which becomes a showcase for Dunsterville's classical guitar solo. The same recording is also included on the four-CD *The Myths and Legends of Rick Wakeman* box set released in 2022. In late November, Rick saw what he believed to be a UFO in the sky over Florida. It was also witnessed by Roger Newell, but the bassist later reasoned that the object must have been Skylab. Either way, the incident was partly inspirational for the forthcoming album Rick was writing.

A handful of dates in Brazil followed and Rick was staggered by the reception he received from the waiting crowds at Rio de Janeiro airport. He was one of the first rock musicians to tour the country and by his estimation, there was an audience of 35,000 at each performance. He was backed by the Brazilian Symphony Orchestra and Choir courtesy of the Brazilian government, who Rick described in his autobiography *Say Yes!* as: 'Absolutely brilliant!' Following the last show in Rio on 21 December, where Rick included a medley from *Lisztomania*, he and his entourage returned home to the cooler climes of the UK, just in time for Christmas.

1976 - Heaven and Earth

...The album has created more controversy than any other album I
have made.
Rick's verdict of *No Earthly Connection* on his website RWCC.

As 1976 dawned, Rick was under pressure from all sides. Despite the
successful tour, he had financial, managerial, and personal problems,
although he kept these mostly to himself. As far as his band were
concerned, it was business as usual. Any hopes that his latest album
would be on the same ambitious scale as his previous projects were
thwarted when manager Brian Lane informed Rick that A&M had
decided there would be no orchestra or choir and he was to record with
the band only. They also vetoed any thoughts of it being a double album
on the grounds that it would reduce sales.

Rick Wakeman - No Earthly Connection

Personnel:
Rick Wakeman: Mander pipe organ, Hammond C3 organ, 9' Steinway
grand piano, RMI Electra piano, Hohner clavinet, Moog synthesizer, Baldwin
electric harpsichord, upright honky-tonk piano, Fender Rhodes 88 electric
piano, Mellotron, Godwin organ with Sisme Rotary-Cabinet, Systech effects
pedals
English Rock Ensemble:
Ashley Holt: vocals
Roger Newell: bass guitar, bass pedals, vocals
John Dunsterville: acoustic and electric guitars, mandolin, vocals
Tony Fernandez: drums, percussion
Martyn Shields: trumpet, flugelhorn, French horn, vocals
Reg Brooks: trombone, bass trombone, vocals
Produced at Château d'Hérouville, France by Rick Wakeman
Recording date: January - March 1976
Release date: April 1976
Record label: A&M
Highest chart places: UK: 9, USA: 67, Australia: 35
Running time: 42:13
All songs and music written by Rick Wakeman
Side one: Music Reincarnate: (20:24): Part I: The Warning, Part II: The
Maker, Part III: The Spaceman, Part IV: The Realisation. Side two: 1. Music

Reincarnate (continued): Part V: The Reaper (7:34), 2. The Prisoner (7:00), 3. The Lost Cycle (7:00)

Following the down-to-earth, historical themes of the previous albums, *No Earthly Connection* saw Rick venture into the spiritual, semi-autobiographical realms normally inhabited by songwriters like Jon Anderson. Following his heart attack in 1974, he had spent several weeks in hospital pondering his own mortality. As such, the fifth album is one of his most personal in its exploration of death, the inner soul and reincarnation. He combines his own Christian faith with elements of fantasy, including a dimension-hopping spaceman and music as an inner life force. The album title reflects the subject of the unknown and in the liner notes, Rick offers this explanation:

All the music is based on a futuristic, autobiographical look at music, the part that it plays in our pre-earth, human and afterlife. Accepting that music is incorporated in our souls, it is up to the individual body in which it lives to nurture and develop this unearthly sense as he is told, in order that upon its return, another life may use it to advance the only true sense in this world of No Earthly Connection.

The inner artwork also features images of Rick leaping over Stonehenge and the Cerne Abbas Giant hill carving in Dorset. The original LP sleeve included a sheet of reflective plastic which, when rolled into a tube and stood on the middle of the album cover, mirrored the distorted painting of Rick as a three-dimensional image.

Rick wrote a good deal of *No Earthly Connection* on the previous tour of America and Brazil, often on the hired jet between cities, scoring it as he went. When he and the band returned to England, they began rehearsals. Unlike many rock musicians, Rick is musically literate and when the melodies came to him, he wrote them down using music notation and scribbled the words in a notebook. He wrote so much before playing it that around 60 per cent was not used. Interviewed for *Yes Music Circle* in 1993, Roger Newell gave an insight into Rick's methods:

What happened to *No Earthly Connection* was that it was never finished. When we started rehearsing it, it was to be a double album. This really was the beginning of the breakup, thinking about it. We went out to France to record it and we had enough material pre-rehearsed for about three-quarters of the single album; the rest of it was to be worked on while we were there. Rick used to have strange ways of working – half of that album we put down without even knowing what the tune was. So, the tune evolved over what we put down; although Rick had got it all in his head, he hadn't played a note of it. Rick knew what the end result was going to be. He could hear it all up in his head, but we first heard it when it was finished. So, we really had a tough job to do, but it was a super band, I mean shit hot players. It was great!

Newell's comments mirror Bill Bruford's recollections of the *Close to the Edge* sessions with no clear indication of what the finished piece would sound like. It was typical of the method in which long-form pieces were assembled. In 1997, guitarist Martin Barre recalled his experience of recording Jethro Tull's 1972 *Thick as a Brick*: 'I don't think we were ever aware what direction the music would end up going in – it was just something that we did on a day-to-day basis'. Echoing his comments, Andy Latimer, interviewed in *Prog* by Mike Barnes in 2015 said of Camel's 1975 *Music Inspired by The Snow Goose*: 'It was a strange album in as much as we recorded all the parts separately, so we didn't know what we had until we edited it all together in the studio'.

Although Rick wrote all the words and music for *No Earthly Connection*, when it came to the arrangements, his mutual respect for the band meant that he would often allow them a degree of flexibility in their interpretation. This was particularly true of Newell, who devised his own bass lines. The brass parts, however, were written out by Rick on manuscript. The band from the previous tour remained intact, apart from percussionist John Hodgson. Ironically, in a band renowned for their drinking prowess, he had to be let go due to an alcohol problem. It was, in Rick's opinion, the finest line-up of the English Rock Ensemble and in many respects, *No Earthly Connection* is a more cogent progressive rock album than his previous two albums, where the absence of an orchestra allows the band to shine. There is also a greater emphasis on the vocal arrangements and for his part, Rick plays a battery of no less than twelve keyboards.

The album was recorded at the infamous Château d'Hérouville studios near Paris, which became a favourite hideaway for many acts in the 1970s, including Elton John, Pink Floyd and David Bowie, all seeking inspiration for their next masterwork. For Rick, it was an appropriate location given that in the nineteenth century, the château was frequented by composer and pianist Frédéric Chopin. Speaking to biographer Dan Wooding, Rick identified the root of his musical inspiration:

The catalyst is the classical side, which produces what comes out. But I'm not trying to make rock fans interested in classical music. I've been lucky. My music's broken all rules with its classical influence and all the orchestras I've used – but it has sold...Everyone has different views about what I should do – a rock keyboard, piano, or classical album. Some think I should include lyrics, while others don't. I listen – and then ignore them.

No Earthly Connection most definitely includes lyrics, as exemplified by the 28-minute 'Music Reincarnate' suite. Although divided into five parts, it plays as one continuous piece, except for the final part which, due to the constraints of vinyl, opens side two. Part one clocks in at around eight minutes, while parts two, three and four average four minutes apiece. 'Part I: The Warning' chronicles the birth of a child and how a young person's thoughts are shaped by the influences around them. It opens with spacey, electronic effects that dissolve into Mellotron strings and multitracked Minimoogs simulating a sustained pipe organ chord, clearly inspired by the dying seconds of Richard Strauss' famous opening theme to 'Also Sprach Zarathustra'. Strident brass, rhythmic electric piano and a distorted bass riff are bookended by inspired vocal sections, including a Gregorian-like a cappella chant and superb counterpoint harmonies led by Ashley Holt. It recalls the madrigal vocal style of Gentle Giant, who toured with Rick the previous year.

'Part II: The Maker' features a lush piano ballad celebrating the 'music of my soul' with synth decorations, a memorable brass theme and Mellotron strings. The sound of running water that leads into 'Part III: The Spaceman' appears innocuous until you realise it was produced by the band relieving themselves into a metal bathtub after drinking several bottles of wine at Château d'Hérouville. It's a rousing song that recalls 'The Battle' from *Journey* with the 'take me to your leader' vocal hook driven by brass, electric piano and lively Minimoog soloing. 'Part IV: The Realisation' features the protagonist in his twilight years acknowledging the mistakes he's made – 'It's too late to find your music soul'. Holt's singing is suitably anguished, but despite the song's downbeat message, it boasts a triumphant brassy instrumental bridge.

'Music Reincarnate' spills over onto side two, concluding with 'Part V: The Reaper'. It incorporates contrasting sections and time signatures and reprises vocal sequences from side one that appear and fade like recurring memories from the past. Newell's bass is once again prominent, as is a metallic rhythmic loop and there is a nice touch of Mellotron flutes at the start. There's a sense of growing anticipation and the final vocal melody tells of a 'music soul rebirth'. Rick lets fly with another Moog solo and finally, the spacey effects and simulated pipe organ return from part one to bring 'Music Reincarnate' full circle.

The theme of 'Music Reincarnate' continues in the two final tracks. 'The Prisoner' opens with John Barry-like staccato brass stabs and a soaring synth theme backed by Mellotron strings. In the verses, the protagonist has committed a 'self-inflicted crime' and in the strident chorus, he is told, 'You shall hang' underlined by a manic organ break. In contrast, the song features some lovely vocal harmonies and Rick finds room for lively electric harpsichord soloing. Like 'The Realisation', 'The Prisoner' had staying power as a stage song that Rick would return to in later years.

'The Lost Cycle' features a strong, synth-led instrumental intro with Tony Fernandez leading with his snares, à la Bill Bruford. The song tells of the missing link in evolution and the influence of a spaceman from a distant civilization. There are obvious parallels with the books by Swiss author Erich von Däniken including *Chariots of the Gods?* which was popular in the 1970s. Rippling, classically tinged piano brings *The Six Wives* to mind, lurching into honky tonk mode at the halfway mark. A disconcerting, backward section follows where the song seems to go into reverse before a massed choral coda provides the requisite grand finale.

Despite variable reviews at the time, *No Earthly Connection* sold more than three million copies and, in May, was another top ten album in the UK, spending nine weeks in the chart. Australia and several European countries remained loyal, although in the USA, it was the start of diminishing returns. Looking back in 2012, Dave Ling in *Classic Rock* commented:

Backed by two of the bandmates who helped to make *Journey to the Centre of the Earth* so successful – namely vocalist Ashely Holt and bassist Roger Newell – Wakeman tempers complex musicianship with a welcome sense of the listenable to voice the album's metaphysical theme, which came in unflinching defiance of the era's musical climate.

Rick was not alone in tackling otherworldly subjects in 1976. *Olias of Sunhillow* by Jon Anderson, *2112* by Rush, *Rising* by Rainbow, *Technical Ecstasy* by Black Sabbath, *Wind & Wuthering* by Genesis, *3:47 EST* by Klaatu, *L* by Steve Hillage, *Rocket Cottage* by Steeleye Span, *Astounding Sounds, Amazing Music* by Hawkwind and the eponymous debut albums from Boston and Starcastle all embrace science fiction and fantasy imagery in the songs and/or album artwork.

The Earthly Tour

In 1974 and 1975, Rick had played a handful of prestigious concerts in the UK, but the first leg of the *No Earthly Connection* tour was his first proper jaunt around his homeland. The sell-out tour visited 26 UK cities and although he had downsized to provincial halls and theatres, it was a welcome opportunity for fans to see him perform outside the capital. The tour programme played down the new album, opting for a humorous football theme instead.

Although the polyphonic Polymoog was introduced in 1976, Rick toured with four Minimoogs, with a spare in case of breakdowns. Normally his rig included two Minimoogs, but he doubled up for one section of music where he couldn't turn around quickly enough without interrupting the flow. He also had a grand piano which had to be tuned before every performance. The tour opened in Bournemouth on 12 April and the following day's concert was captured on tape for the *Rick at Hemel Hempstead* bootleg. One week later, your author caught up with Rick and his band at the De Montfort Hall in Leicester. Three consecutive nights at London's legendary Hammersmith Odeon followed and in the *Daily Telegraph* newspaper John Constable enthused:

Judging by the enormously popular and impeccably produced concert at the Hammersmith Odeon, economic stringency has done Rick Wakeman a great service. No longer do we have inflatable monsters fighting in lakes or mediaeval knights duelling on Wembley's ice. In their place this most accessible of 'superstar' musicians has substituted a more modest, but razor-sharp programme of his best compositions, performed with a sextet, the English Rock Ensemble, who have improved beyond all measure since last year's excesses. Wakeman never forgot his credo that entertainment is all. If the title extract from *Journey to the Centre of the Earth* seemed too weighty an opening, the ribald spoken introductions and the excellent John Dunsterville's self-parody of a classical guitar solo were the perfect levellers. Even the road crew were given a pantomime spot to open the second half.

On 27 April, Rick staged a performance at the Farnham Maltings for BBC TV's *The Old Grey Whistle Test* and on 17 June, he returned by popular demand to the Hammersmith Odeon and was recorded for the BBC Radio One *In Concert* series. The Maltings recording was released as the *Live on the Test* CD in 1994 and both shows appeared on the two-CD *Live at the BBC* in 2007 and *The Myths and Legends of Rick Wakeman* box set in 2022. Both recordings feature three pieces from *No Earthly Connection* along with a selection from the previous albums, but they do not include the full setlist. Two 1976 stage favourites are missing; 'Anne Boleyn', which Rick would end with a flourish of 'Rhapsody in Blue' and 'Hungarian Rhapsody No.13'.

On 10 May, without a pause, the tour steamed through mainland Europe taking in the Netherlands, Sweden, Denmark, Germany, Belgium, Austria, Switzerland, France, and Spain. Looking back, Rick later reflected: 'The whole tour had been a smash. After performing so much in North and South America as well as Japan, Australia, and New Zealand, it was a knockout to be able to play in Europe again'.

During the *No Earthly Connection* tour, Rick had begun work on his second film soundtrack, *White Rock*, a documentary of the 1976 Winter Olympics. Only drummer Tony Fernandez from the English Rock Ensemble was involved and during the European leg, Rick made several flights back to London to work on the score.

After the final date headlining the Jazz Bilzen festival in Belgium on 13 August, Rick returned home. The UK was basking in the long hot summer of 1976, but Rick had other things on his mind. He found mounting debts waiting for him and despite the success of the tour, he was out of pocket to the tune of £350,000. It was no longer viable to maintain a full-time band and he disbanded the English Rock Ensemble. Rick had hoped that the band would continue for at least five years, but, for the time being, at least, that wasn't to be. He acknowledged in his 1978 biography that it was the hardest task he had to do at that point in his career.

Understandably, the ERE members were upset and disillusioned with the sudden break-up of the band. Rick offered to sell bassist Roger Newell the Wal triple-neck guitar, but he was unable to pay the asking price of £1,000. The following year, drummer Tony Fernandez joined

Rick's old band, Strawbs. Looking back in 1993, Newell remained philosophical:

Rick believed in what he did, and he gave the public what he thought they wanted and you mustn't knock people for that. He did it with all integrity. He did it for the right reasons.

It wasn't all bad news for Rick; he and the members of Yes once again showed a clean pair of heels to the competition in the annual *Melody Maker* reader's poll. While Rick deserved such plaudits, let's not forget that the 1970s was a watershed period for keyboard players, some of whom, like Rick, were classically trained. During the 1960s, most rock groups were limited to guitar, bass, and drums, where piano and organ – when required – were provided by a session musician. At the turn of the decade, progressive rock bands in particular expanded their instrumental palette, and the role of the keyboardist became more clearly defined.

Like Rick, Tony Banks of Genesis utilised multiple keyboards, although his stage rig was more modest and his synthesiser of choice was the ARP Pro Soloist, first used on *Selling England by the Pound* (1973). Unlike both musicians, Keith Emerson shunned the Mellotron in favour of his bulky modular Moog, creating some very convincing orchestral sounds on *Trilogy* (1972). For Mike Pinder of The Moody Blues, however, Mellotron was his lead instrument of choice, embellishing several lush ballads on *Seventh Sojourn* (1972). Another notable Mellotron practitioner was Wolly Wolstenholme of Barclay James Harvest. In addition to piano, Rick admired Emerson for his Hammond organ talents, as he did Jon Lord of Deep Purple, while other skilled exponents include Thijs Van Leer of Dutch band Focus. Greek virtuoso Vangelis combined a variety of synths with piano and percussion for his immersive soundscapes, evident on the impressive *Heaven and Hell* (1975). Like his predecessor John Hawken, Renaissance keyboardist John Tout's preferred instrument was piano, and his classical style graced memorable albums like *Turn of the Cards* (1974). Formed in 1972, Greenslade took the unconventional step of fronting the band with two keyboardists – Dave Greenslade, who played organ, Mellotron and piano and Dave Lawson, who handled synth and electric piano as well as lead vocals.

Unfortunately for Rick, accolades do not pay the bills and to generate ready cash, he sold off his non-musical interests, including the luxury car hire business Fragile Carriage Company and his fleet of vintage cars. A lifeline came from A&M Records, who agreed to pay Rick royalties ahead of future record sales. Manager Brian Lane also sought other outlets that would put Rick's bank balance back on track. This included a union with drummer Bill Bruford and bassist John Wetton – free from a disbanded King Crimson – and the trio rehearsed for six weeks. On 16 October, *Melody Maker* leaked the news and the contractual complications that followed ended any hope of forming a supergroup. According to Bruford, Rick was also reluctant to commit.

As manager of both Rick and Yes, it wouldn't have escaped Lane's notice of another possibility that would solve the keyboardist's monetary problems. If financial inducement from his record company had played a part in luring Rick away from Yes two years earlier; money, or rather the lack of it, would also be a factor when he rekindled his relationship in 1976.

Never Say Never Again

In Rick's absence, the five members of Yes followed his 1973 lead and between October 1975 and July 1976, they released their debut solo albums. At the end of August, Yes returned home from a triumphant three-month trek around North America. They had played in some of the biggest arenas of their career, including a Bicentennial concert at Philadelphia's JFK Stadium to a record-breaking crowd of 130,000.

For the next album, they decided to forsake the London studios and head for the tax haven of Switzerland and Mountain Studios in Montreux. In theory, it was an ideal location for keyboardist Patrick Moraz who was on home turf, even though he was then living in Brazil. After a few weeks of rehearsals, however, he found himself out in the cold. A lack of communication and musical affinity was blamed on both sides and in *Yes: The Authorised Biography*, Moraz claimed:

> With Yes, I realised that they always keep the keyboards very subdued in the mix. Whether there's a keyboard player there or not doesn't really matter unless it's Rick Wakeman, because he has that charisma. But I never felt there was an important relationship between the keyboards and the other instruments in Yes. I had no responsibilities.

His feelings are perhaps understandable, given that he'd been sidelined. Even so, his keyboards are prominent on the *Relayer* album, and he had a conspicuous stage presence with Yes, both visually and instrumentally. He clearly had the respect of his colleagues in the band because he guests on both Steve Howe's and Chris Squire's debut solo albums. His comments do, however, illustrate that even for a talented keyboardist like Moraz, filling Rick's shoes was a daunting prospect.

In early November, Brian Lane's partner and tour manager, Alex Scott, contacted Rick with a view to him joining the band in Montreux. Jon Anderson was understandably reticent, as was Rick, given his verbal assault on *Topographic Oceans* nearly three years earlier. When Rick heard the demos the band had recorded, he felt it was a return to the spontaneity and style that had attracted him to Yes in the first place and he definitely wanted in. Interviewed in *Yes: The Authorised Biography*, he reflected:

> The irony of it all is that Jon and I realised that we were really after the same thing. It's just that with our different backgrounds and influences, we were trying for it in our own way. That goes for the others too, I think. I've said this before, but if you can imagine this big sphere, with all of us on one side trying to get around to the other side…we might go in different directions to get there, but we're all aiming for that exact same place on the other side.

He was initially hired as a session musician, but during a party thrown by Warner Bros' European boss and Montreux Jazz Festival founder Claude Nobs, Chris Squire suggested to Rick that he join the band as a full-time member. He reasoned that as Rick played on the album and knew the material, he would have to come out on the road with them. Rick agreed and when the news reached London, *Melody Maker* ran the front-page headline: 'Wakeman Rejoins Yes'. It was the 4 December and for many Yes fans, Christmas 1976 had arrived three weeks early. There was a renewed energy and vibe within the band, as Alan White confirmed in the *Yesyears* video in 1991:

> It was such a happy period in the band's life when Rick came back to the fold and was playing really great – I think there's some really creative moments. And that's what the album means to me, the joining back to the fold of Rick Wakeman and the happiness of all that.

1977 – The Return of the Prodigal Son

Going for the One came along and I thought, yeah, this is an album I
can get involved with.
Rick interviewed for the *Toronto Star* in March 2022.

1977 was Rick and Yes' most productive year of the latter half of the
1970s. As was typical of the band, the recording of their eighth studio
album was a painstaking process and the sessions continued into spring.
Just a few weeks into the year, Rick had an album of his own to unveil,
which would prove to be an unexpected delight.

Rick Wakeman – White Rock

Personnel:
Rick Wakeman: Moog synthesiser, Steinway grand piano, Mellotron,
Mander pipe organ, RMI Computer Piano, marimba, RMI Rock-Si-Chord,
Hohner clavinet, Fender Rhodes piano, Hammond C3 organ, grand piano
Tony Fernandez: drums, percussion
St Paul's Cathedral Choir
Produced at Cine-Tele Sound Studios, The Music Centre, Wembley and
Advision Studios, London by Rick Wakeman
Recording date: January – September 1976
Release date: January 1977
Record label: A&M
Highest chart places: UK: 14, USA: 126, Australia: 38
Running time: 34:52
All tracks written by Rick Wakeman except as noted otherwise
Side one: 1. White Rock (3:10), 2. Searching for Gold (4:20), 3. The Loser
(5:30), 4. The Shoot (3:59). Side two: 1. Lax'x (4:53), 2. After the Ball (3:03), 3.
Montezuma's Revenge (3:56) (traditional), 4. Ice Run (6:11)

When Yes were approached to provide the music for the official
film documentary of the 1976 Winter Olympics, they turned it down.
Fortunately for Rick, he and Yes shared the same manager and Brian
Lane passed the option to him. Despite his disillusionment over the way
Lisztomania had turned out, he accepted. Rick had the film's producer
Michael Samuelson to thank, explaining in *Classic Rock* magazine in
2012: '...He was fed up with hearing orchestral music or brass band
music on sports films and it was time for rock 'n' roll to make an entry'.

Samuelson and director Tony Maylam had seen the TV film of *King Arthur* on ice and were suitably impressed. The Olympics were staged in Innsbruck, Austria, from the 4 to 15 February and rather than attempting a compressive overview, Maylam focuses on specific events to contrast the drama and excitement with the beauty and grace of the games. Hollywood actor James Coburn, better known for his tough guy roles, was hired as the narrator.

Work on *White Rock* was spread over a protracted period to accommodate the *No Earthly Connection* tour. The scoring process began with a preview screening of the film, where Rick noted the points at which the music should be inserted on a timing sheet. The producer and director gave him an outline of the style of music required for each scene. Rick was able to complement the visuals with a variety of interpretations, from synthesised rock to lush melodies. When the writing and arrangements were complete, Rick spent five weeks recording the mostly instrumental soundtrack, which was precisely timed to match the action on the screen. It was scored at CTS in Wembley, where many of the major film composers of the day recorded, including John Barry and Jerry Goldsmith.

As is often the case with film soundtracks, the music was rearranged and remixed for the album. Following rehearsals with drummer Tony Fernandez which often turned into lengthy jam sessions, Rick recorded in the familiar surroundings of London's Advision Studios with engineer Paul Hardiman. He adapted and added to the score so that it would succeed as a standalone album.

The title track provides a suitably spirited introduction with a dazzling Moog fanfare that recalls Keith Emerson in both speed and timbre. It launches into something akin to a 12-bar blues shuffle and Rick's speed and agility is jaw-dropping, worthy of the downhill skiers on the screen. In contrast, 'Searching for Gold' is a wistful piece, accompanying the graceful, aerial flight of the ski jumping. Piano and synth are tempered by the ethereal timbre of the St Paul's Cathedral Choir. In keeping with the title, 'The Loser' is a melancholic piece with piano arpeggios overlaid with heavenly synth string washes and choir. A change of mood for 'The Shoot', a regal offering featuring a glorious synth melody with a touch of Fender Rhodes, Mellotron strings, organ, and a funky clavinet interlude.

Opening side two of the vinyl LP, 'Lax'x' is like nothing else in Rick's output in the 1970s. Fernandez is prominent and his high-hat loop provides the rhythmic undercurrent, joined by random electric piano chords, percussion, and a sultry synth waltz. Dive-bombing synth lines introduce piano and a delightful little pipe organ theme. Although Rick had a dislike for *Topographic Oceans*, the section beginning at 4:10 recalls a sequence from Yes' 'Ritual', beginning around the 16:10 mark, where frantic Moog and Mellotron similarly spiral skywards. The propulsive drum pattern is also similar to Alan White's.

White Rock producer Samuelson was a fan of Franz Liszt and asked Rick to write a piano piece in the style of 'Liebestraum' ('Love Dream'). 'After the Ball' was the result, an elegant tone poem to complement the ice skaters. For the album, Rick added synth, which takes up the melody at 1:10 with piano playing counterpoint. As a solo piano piece, 'After the Ball' became one of Rick's most popular stage numbers. As you might expect from the title, the penultimate 'Montezuma's Revenge' is a light-hearted romp that could be best described as a synth rock version of a gypsy folk dance.

The concluding 'Ice Run' is another multi-faceted piece, featuring inventive orchestrations. It opens with a lyrical synth melody, underscored by rhythmic piano. Crashing cymbals at 1:35 herald the entrance of the majestic Mander pipe organ and the free-falling Mellotron lines beginning at 2:53 are dazzling. At 3:30, clavinet and a syncopated rhythm take a rockier direction and the jazzy Hammond solo beginning at 4:28 is simply stunning.

Arguably, Rick's music was influential, where even today, a sports review on TV is often accompanied by rock music. The album was released in January to coincide with the release of the film and entered the UK chart on 12 February, where it spent nine weeks. Film soundtracks rarely sell this well unless they include a hit song or popular theme tune. The film itself was nominated for a BAFTA award in 1977. In 1997, Rick was approached to score a re-edited TV transmission of the 1976 Winter Olympics, which he released as *White Rock II* in 1999. In *The Caped Crusader* biography, writer-director Tony Maylam acknowledged Rick's talents:

Rick is no ordinary rock musician. His deep understanding of all aspects of music means he has been able to develop a further dimension in his work; a depth that is often lacking in the music of his contemporaries. His score for *White Rock* has contributed substantially to the film experience.

The UK critics generally agreed with Maylam's assessment. Both the music and the camera work, shot in widescreen Panavision, were innovative, which many viewers were quick to recognise. In his review of the film in the *Daily Mirror* newspaper, Arthur Thirkell wrote: 'Rock musician Rick Wakeman's score, using keyboard, percussion and choral themes, heightens the drama in a superb documentary'.

White Rock was part of a double feature with *Genesis: In Concert* which was also directed by Maylam. The latter was filmed during the band's 1976 UK tour with Phil Collins out front for the first time and the drum stool occupied by Rick's ex-bandmate Bill Bruford. On Monday, 31 January, Rick attended the Royal Premiere at the ABC theatre on London's Shaftesbury Avenue. Prior to the screening, he was introduced to Princess Anne, who, six months earlier, had competed in the 1976 Summer Olympics. No sooner had Rick returned home and taken off his black tie, he was on a flight back to Switzerland to continue work on his fourth studio album with Yes.

Yes – Going for the One

Personnel:

Jon Anderson: lead vocals, harp

Steve Howe: steel guitar, acoustic and electric guitars, vachalia, pedal steel guitar, vocals

Chris Squire: bass guitar, fretless bass, 8-string bass, vocals

Rick Wakeman: piano, electric keyboards, church organ at St. Martin's in Vevey, Polymoog synthesizer, choral arrangement on 'Awaken'

Alan White: drums, percussion, tuned percussion

Additional personnel:

Ars Laeta of Lausanne: choir on 'Awaken'

Richard Williams Singers: choir on 'Awaken'

Produced at Mountain Studios, Montreux, Switzerland by Yes

Recording date: October 1976 – April 1977

Release date: 15 July 1977

Record label: Atlantic

Highest chart places: UK: 1, USA: 8, Canada: 8

Running time: 38:43

Side one: 1. Going for the One (5:30) (Jon Anderson), 2. Turn of the Century (7:58) (Anderson, Steve Howe, Alan White), 3. Parallels (5:52) (Chris Squire). Side two: 1. Wonderous Stories (3:45) (Anderson), 2. Awaken (15:38) (Anderson, Howe)

Although Yes had elected to record *Going for the One* in Montreux as a tax avoidance measure, they lived the highlife during their stay, including fine apartments, parties, daily skiing, and racing hired cars around Lake Geneva. Rick's accountant advised him to stay in Switzerland for a full year as a tax exile and he was soon entrenched in the lifestyle. Rosaline remained in the UK with their two children and she and Rick divorced in 1977, ending their seven-year marriage.

A typical working day in Mountain Studios began at 1.00 pm. As it's a relatively small studio, Yes rehearsed in the downstairs casino. Following the *Relayer* album in 1974, Yes had found Eddie Offord increasingly difficult to work with and as a result, *Going for the One* was produced by the band, assisted by experienced recording engineer John Timperley. He does an admirable job, but the production is perhaps the album's Achilles heel. Given the complexity and density of the band's arrangements, it lacks the sonic clarity that Eddie Offord brought to their previous studio albums. Offord also knew how to get the best out of the band and marshal their individual contributions into a cohesive whole.

Patrick Moraz contributed to the material prior to his departure, but he was never credited. When he joined Yes in 1974, he was warmly accepted by fans, especially during live performances, but understandably, Rick's return was greeted with elation. In his autobiography, *Say Yes!* Rick states that nothing had been recorded for *Going for the One* prior to his arrival. Like Moraz, he doesn't receive any writing credits, although his contributions to tracks like 'Turn of the Century' and 'Awaken' are considerable. In a radio interview in June 1977, Rick enthused: 'The album gives me the same buzz that *Fragile* and *Close to the Edge* gave me and more. Excellent album'.

In addition to the quality of the material, a key factor in the album's success is its diversity. *Going for the One* is Yes' most eclectic offering since *Fragile* in 1971, covering many different tones and styles. It opens with the rousing title song, followed by the neoclassical romanticism of 'Turn of the Century' and Chris Squire's rocking 'Parallels'.

Although side two contains just two songs, the lyrical 'Wonderous Stories' is one of Jon Anderson's most accessible offerings, while 'Awaken' is an undisputed epic in the tradition of 'Close to the Edge'. Also, for the first time since *The Six Wives of Henry VIII*, Rick found himself in church for part of the recording.

He introduces the Polymoog synthesiser on this album which he would also play on *Criminal Record* and *Tormato*. Launched in 1975 by the Moog company, it was a pioneering polyphonic analogue instrument and although it was popular with keyboardists at the time, it was notoriously expensive and unreliable. A polyphonic – as opposed to monophonic – instrument, multiple notes could be played simultaneously on the 71-note keyboard. Like all of Rick's electronic instruments at the time, the settings were modified to his requirements by keyboard technician Toby Errington before taking it out on the road.

'Going for the One' is a 'Roundabout' for the late 1970s. Following Alan White's count-in, it's off the starting blocks like a thoroughbred led by searing steel guitar underpinned by Polymoog and rhythmic piano. It's an adrenaline rush, replete with sporting metaphors and Anderson's self-reflective lines 'So I'm thinking I should go and write a punchline, but they're so hard to find in my cosmic mind'. Rick's lively synth almost spirals out of control before the repeated choral refrain 'Love' brings the song to a breathless close. A 3:40 version was the second single release from the album and although it didn't capture the public's imagination in the same way as 'Wonderous Stories', it reached number 24 in the UK on 3 December 1977. The B side is a 6:40 edit of 'Awaken Pt. 1'.

'Turn of the Century' is an oft-forgotten gem that contains some of Anderson's most poetic lyrics, relating the story of a sculptor who seemingly brings his deceased partner back to life. His vocal is suitably dreamy, and the instrumentation and arrangement are lush with acoustic guitar and layered keyboard strings. The song is bridged at 3:50 by a glorious instrumental interlude featuring a piano and weeping guitar duet before the bittersweet vocal sequence beginning 'Was the sign in the day with a touch, as I kiss your fingers'. With Howe's guitar soaring skywards, it still has the power to send shivers down the spine. White had begun using piano to write around the *Topographic Oceans* period and his input to this song is substantial.

'Parallels' is a leftover from Squire's 1975 solo album *Fish Out of Water*. Along with its other qualities, it proves that in the hands of Rick, a church organ can rock. It was played at St. Martin's church in Vevey, nine kilometres from Montreux, and at Timperley's suggestion, relayed into Mountain Studios via Switzerland's high-fidelity telephone system. The song celebrates the power of love with a zestful spring in its step, driven by Squire's propulsive bass and White's relentless drumming. Howe's guitar goes into overdrive and Rick's inspired solo at 3:28 must have shaken the church walls to their foundation.

'Parallels' was the UK B side of the 'Wonderous Stories' single released in September 1977. It spent nine weeks in the top 40, peaking at number seven on 8 October. It remains Yes' only UK top twenty single and their highest charting internationally until 'Owner of a Lonely Heart' topped the American chart in January 1984. During the 1970s, a hit single from a successful albums band was a welcome bonus and the appeal of 'Wonderous Stories' is obvious, particularly Anderson's multi-tracked vocals. Like 'Turn of the Century', White is responsible for the chords, and the sprightly arrangement features Howe's 12-string Portuguese acoustic and Rick's cascading Polymoog lines.

'Awaken' was assembled in five parts and at its heart is a three-and-a-half-minute harp and pipe organ duet backed by tuned percussion and choir, which Rick and Jon would improvise on the subsequent tour. It's Yes at their most tastefully understated, as is the descending piano arpeggio and hymnal 'High vibration go on' theme that opens the song. Howe's towering electric 12-string solo is supported by the agile rhythm and during the tour, Squire played the Wal custom triple-neck guitar inherited from the English Rock Ensemble. During the instrumental sequence at 4:35, Rick switches from synth to organ with equal dexterity. The potent climax with monumental organ chords, pedal steel guitar and choral arrangement is Yes at their majestic best, recalling 'And You and I' from five years earlier. The coda featuring a reprise of the 'High vibration go on' theme with swirling keyboard effects is sublime. It remains a favourite of both Rick and Jon Anderson and for many fans, it ranks second only to 'Close to the Edge' as Yes' finest achievement. Rick's enthusiasm remained some 25 years later when quoted in the programme for the European leg of Yes' *Full Circle Tour*:

'Awaken' has to stand for me as being the epitome of what Yes stands for. Add to that the *Fragile* and *Close to the Edge* albums and you're almost there. There was some great stuff on *Tormato* and I loved *90125* as well. But 'Awaken' was something really special from the moment it started to take shape in the studio in Switzerland. There were so many elements that made up this track that it could merit its own book on how it came to be. 'Awaken' was a musical vision that came from within. It was a very special musical moment in Yes history.

Critics were equally enthusiastic, although John Swenson's review in *Rolling Stone* in September 1977 was more guarded than most:

By letting the Chris Squire-Alan White rhythm section construct a bottom for Howe's guitar and by using Wakeman's unquestionable keyboard talent intelligently, *Going for the One* takes the right step towards downplaying Anderson's conceptual stranglehold on the band.

On 13 August, four weeks after its release, *Going for the One* reached the top of the UK chart, Yes' second number one album of the 1970s. Until late February 1978, it languished for 28 weeks in the top 60, its staying power no doubt aided by the success of the two singles. It was a global hit, scaling the top 20 in the USA, Canada, Japan, Australasia, Scandinavia, and all over Europe.

Due to a disagreement between the band and Roger Dean, Hipgnosis was commissioned for the album artwork. Dean's familiar Yes logo is present and correct, but otherwise the cover is sleek and modern, reflecting the changing musical climate of the times. Skyscrapers tower above a naked man, the third nude figure to appear on a Yes album cover in the 1970s. The original LP sleeve is a trifold design which, when opened, reveals images of the band members by Lake Geneva, where they spent recreational time in between recording.

Going for the One was released in a transitional musical climate where the album charts on both sides of the Atlantic reflected the diversity of popular acts, including Queen, Iggy Pop, Pink Floyd, Meat Loaf, David Bowie, Supertramp, Kiss, Ian Dury, The Alan Parsons Project, Steely Dan, The Clash, Journey, and The Sex Pistols.

Going for the Tour

Sales of *Going for the One* in America were boosted by the first leg of the *Yesshows World Tour 1977,* supported by Donavon. They opened at the Toledo Sports Arena in Ohio on 30 July and with a further 54-dates, it was Yes' most demanding hike around North America yet. In the Yes stronghold of Philadelphia, 40,000 tickets were sold in less than a day. The stage set was less elaborate than previous outings, but nonetheless striking in its angular simplicity. 'Parallels' proved to be a rousing show owner, following in the footsteps of 'Siberian Khatru' and 'Sound Chaser'.

On the tour, Rick replaced his double Mellotron set-up with the recently developed Birotron which he had financed. Like the Mellotron, it replicates the sound of orchestral instruments and choral voices using pre-recorded tapes triggered by the keys. Mellotron tapes play for just eight seconds and experienced players like Rick, Mike Pinder and Tony Banks developed techniques to sustain string sounds. The Birotron's eight-track tape loops played indefinitely and when it was marketed in 1976, it was in high demand from notable musicians, including Keith Emerson and Vangelis. But development costs spiralled, and very few were manufactured and today, it's renowned as the 'World's rarest musical instrument'. Rick was one of the few musicians to own and play a Birotron, but his investment cost him dearly.

Yes returned to London in October and at the end of the month, they played a record-breaking six sold-out shows at the Empire Pool, Wembley. Earlier in March, Pink Floyd played five dates at the same venue during the *In the Flesh Tour* promoting *Animals*. In *The Sunday Times* on 30 October, Derek Jewell waxed lyrical about the performance in an article suitably titled 'Yes at the summit':

For Yes, Wembley Pool – their haven for six nights and sixty thousand listeners – was an opening night like a cathedral. An audience intent on the music, except when the acolytes were invited to participate, the choral harmonies keening, Rick Wakeman's powerful organ pealing, Jon Anderson's modern countertenor spinning words like psalmist's verses and finally, a forest of arms raised in worship salute…The return to Yes of Rick Wakeman, bearded like the pard (sic), is good for the band and for him. He's not straining so much with his battery of keyboards, content to cement the whole sound together without excessive pyrotechnics.

The Yes faithful demonstrated their loyalty with ticket sales and votes in 1977. Yes scored highly in magazine polls around the world, including topping the *Melody Maker* international band category. Your author caught up with Yes at the Bingley Hall, Stafford, in November and despite the venue's lack of atmosphere, Rick was in tremendous form, particularly during 'Awaken' and 'Parallels' which featured a blistering right-handed Minimoog solo while playing organ with his left. The final leg of the tour took in 23-dates in mainland Europe before finally coming to a halt in Paris on 6 December. If ever a group deserved their Christmas holiday that year, it was Yes. Three songs recorded in Europe in November – 'Parallels', 'Going for the One' and 'Wonderous Stories' – would appear on the *Yesshows* double LP in 1980.

Rick Wakeman's Criminal Record

Personnel:

Rick Wakeman: Steinway 9' grand piano, Minimoog synthesiser, Polymoog synthesiser, Hammond C3 organ, Birotron, Mander pipe organ at St. Martin's church in Vevey, RMI computer keyboard, harpsichord, Fender Rhodes 88 electric piano, Hohner clavinet, Baldwin electric harpsichord

Chris Squire: bass guitar on 'Statue of Justice', 'Crime of Passion' and 'Chamber of Horrors'

Alan White: drums on 'Statue of Justice', 'Crime of Passion' and 'Chamber of Horrors'

Frank Ricotti: percussion on 'Statue of Justice', 'Crime of Passion', 'Chamber of Horrors' and 'Judas Iscariot'

Bill Oddie: vocals on 'The Breathalyser'

Ars Laeta of Lausanne: choir on 'Judas Iscariot'

Robert Mernoud: choir conductor on 'Judas Iscariot'

Produced at Mountain Studios, Montreux, Switzerland by Rick Wakeman

Recording date: April – June 1977

Release date: 9 November 1977

Record label: A&M

Highest chart places: UK: 25, USA: 128, Australia: 76

Running time: 39:04

All tracks written by Rick Wakeman, except as noted otherwise

Side one: 1. Statue of Justice (6:20), 2. Crime of Passion (5:46), 3. Chamber of Horrors (6:40). Side two: 1. Birdman of Alcatraz (4:12), 2. The Breathalyser (3:51) (Rick Wakeman, Montague Ewing), 3. Judas Iscariot (12:15)

Rick's seventh album *Criminal Record* was recorded virtually back-to-back with Yes' *Going for the One* in the same studio with the same engineers, John Timperley, and Dave Richards. In the tradition of *The Six Wives*, it's a concept album that combines six pieces of predominantly instrumental music with crime and punishment as the theme. It's a remarkably self-contained work with three proggy instrumentals, a piano ballad, a novelty song, and a mini-epic to close. On the three tracks that occupy side one, he's supported by two of his recently reunited bandmates.

In an era where the punk rock revolution, new wave and disco fever were at their peak, *Criminal Record* is unashamedly progressive rock where Rick runs the full gamut of his musical talents. Rick had recently voiced his disapproval over A&M Records' signing of the Sex Pistols, who the label dropped like the proverbial hot potato after just one week in March 1977. Although *Criminal Record* is another in a succession of themed albums from Rick, it's a myth that the 1970s was awash with prog rock concept albums, with Yes and Genesis, for example, releasing just one apiece.

Unfortunately for Rick, although the album title may have seemed like a witty pun given the subject, it backfired, providing an all too easy target for naysayers who considered his music out of step with the times. The only thing criminal about the record was the lack of appreciation by the critics and despite its many qualities, it was Rick's lowest chart showing yet. It entered the UK top 100 at a promising 25 on 3 December but, sadly, dropped out after just five weeks. In the USA, it fell short of the *Billboard* top 100, although it did better in many other regions. Paul Elliott, in *Classic Rock* magazine in 2012, identified *Criminal Record* as: 'A high-minded, neo-classical / prog-rock extravaganza, and a concept album to boot, it was the very antithesis of punk's lo-fi idealism'.

Side one featuring Chris Squire and Alan White is possibly the finest 19 minutes of music Yes never recorded. They prove themselves to be a formidable keyboard-led trio to rival Emerson, Lake & Palmer. Rick recorded the keyboards for all three instrumentals and then gave the Yes rhythm engine free licence to arrange the bass and drum parts to fit. As Rick had recorded without a rhythm track, it proved to be a challenge but Squire and White do a sterling job under the circumstances. Famed session musician Frank Ricotti, who played on *The Six Wives*, overdubbed percussion.

Despite the subjects, the music for all three tracks is infectiously uplifting. 'Statue of Justice' begins with a dazzling display of improvised piano virtuosity that Keith Emerson would be proud of. At 2:15, a synth fanfare launches a round of majestic Hammond and Moog soloing, where melody remains front and centre. Grand piano features prominently in 'Crime of Passion', providing the stately opening theme. At 1:55, synth explodes into a colourful display of instrumental pyrotechnics before launching into a funky jazz workout at 2:46. Piano returns to bring the piece to a sublime conclusion. The hyperactive 'Chamber of Horrors' is brimming with musical invention, including a galloping synth theme, a quirky electric piano sequence and vibrant organ playing. White's busy drumming leads the final charge and Squire's sublime coda is followed by a high-pitched scream courtesy of an unnamed Swiss girl that Rick met in a Montreux bar.

Opening side two, 'Birdman of Alcatraz' is one of Rick's most evocative melodies for solo piano, which, surprisingly, he rarely performed live. To produce the overlapping lines, he recorded and layered several different piano tracks. The subject, convicted murderer Robert Stroud, was imprisoned for life, and spent 17 years in the notorious penitentiary in San Francisco Bay. Rick's sensitive playing captures the disparity between Stroud's crimes and his devoted work as an ornithologist. In 1978, the BBC adopted 'Birdman of Alcatraz' as the theme for the TV miniseries *My Son My Son* on the strength of which it was released as a single in 1979.

Like ELP, Rick was prone to the occasional novelty track to lighten the mood, in this case, 'The Breathalyser'. Bill Oddie, who was well known to British television viewers during the 1970s as one-third of the popular comedy trio *The Goodies*, provides the vocals, mimicking a slow, American blues drawl. The electric piano hook is remarkably like 'The Laughing Gnome', a hit for David Bowie in 1967 and at 0:50, it morphs into the vintage 'Policeman's Holiday' by Montague Ewing. Rick concludes with a snippet of the *Dixon of Dock Green* TV theme from the 1950s and 1960s composed by Jeff Darnell.

Although *Criminal Record* did not meet Rick's own expectations, he remains justly proud of the final track, 'Judas Iscariot', which, in some respects, is the natural successor to 'Awaken', which Yes themselves were unable to emulate. Once again, he plays the St. Martin's church pipe organ in Vevey and, likewise, the Ars Laeta of Lausanne choir return, recorded at a church in Les Planches, the old town district of Montreux. The celestial ambience is appropriate given the biblical theme of Judas and his betrayal of Jesus. The combination of piano, pipe organ and Moog is stunning with more than a hint of J. S. Bach and the gothic theme at 8:26 pre-empts Andrew Lloyd Webber's *The Phantom of the Opera* by almost nine years. At 9:36, the choir hums the hymn 'There is a Green Hill Far Away', a moment of serenity before the majestic finale.

The non-gatefold sleeve features a serious, almost sinister-looking Rick sitting at the piano in formal evening dress with a cigar in his left hand and a gavel in his right. On the reverse, there is a dedication to Fabio Nicoli, who was responsible for the art direction on Rick's previous albums and died shortly before the release of *Criminal Record*.

1978 – Ten True Summers

It just seems to me like both Rick and Steve on that particular album (*Tormato)* were seeing which one could play more notes than the other one.
Chris Squire interview – *Notes from the Edge* 1994

1978 marked the tenth anniversary of Yes' formation and Rick's first recording session as a professional musician. In mid-February, the band was deep into rehearsals at Sound Associates by London's Queensway for their ninth studio album. To ensure they had ample material to choose from, they amassed almost enough for a double album, although the quality did not necessarily match the quantity. It was also a familiar scenario where they spent endless hours changing the arrangements of each song, sometimes ending up back where they started. Like Bill Bruford before him, Alan White believed that spontaneity was key and could often result in better music, but Chris Squire remained ever the perfectionist, as he confirmed in *Yes: The Authorised Biography*:

Yeah, maybe I do take a long time. But I can name a lot of albums that, if they'd had that approach to them, would have been a lot better. …When I make a record – and a Yes album is just as much my record as it is everyone else's – I'm thinking about something people will be happy to put on in 50 years' time.

Yes – Tormato
Personnel:
Jon Anderson: vocals, 10-string Alvarez guitar
Steve Howe: Gibson Les Paul Custom guitar, Martin 000–45, Fender Broadcaster, Gibson ES-175, Gibson acoustic guitar, mandolin, Spanish guitar, vocals
Chris Squire: harmonised Rickenbacker bass, Gibson Thunderbird bass, bass pedals, piano, vocals
Rick Wakeman: Birotron, Hammond organ, Polymoog synthesizer, piano, harpsichord, RMI Electra Piano
Alan White: drums, military snare drum, glockenspiel, crotales, cymbals, bell tree, drum synthesizer, gongs, vibraphone, vocals
Produced at Advision Studios and RAK Studios, London by Yes
Recording date: February – June 1978

Release date: 22 September 1978
Record label: Atlantic
Highest chart places: UK: 8, USA: 10, Canada: 30
Running time: 40:57
Side one: 1. Future Times / Rejoice (6:45) (Jon Anderson, Steve Howe, Chris Squire, Rick Wakeman, Alan White), 2. Don't Kill the Whale (3:56) (Anderson, Squire), 3. Madrigal (2:23) (Anderson, Wakeman), 4. Release, Release (5:47) (Anderson, Squire, White). Side two: 1. Arriving UFO (6:03) (Anderson, Howe, Wakeman), 2. Circus of Heaven (4:30) (Anderson), 3. Onward (4:02) (Squire), 4. On the Silent Wings of Freedom (7:47) (Anderson, Squire)

For their ninth studio album, Yes returned to familiar territory – London's Advision Studios – although they again elected to self-produce. The album contains eight tracks – nine if you split the opening pairing – more than any previous Yes studio album post *Fragile*. 1978 was an uncertain musical climate for bands like Yes who, a few years earlier, had been masters of all they surveyed, but were now labelled as dinosaurs. As a result, the songs are more concise with no attempt to create another 'Close to the Edge' or 'Awaken' which, as Chris Squire confirmed in the 1981 Yes biography, took considerable time and effort to perfect: 'It's not easy to work on extended pieces. They need an incredible amount of foresight and arrangement, and the knowledge to encompass them so that they come off well'.

It's generally accepted that *Tormato* lacks clear direction partly due to Jon Anderson's decision to take a step back and not stamp his authority as he had done on previous albums. Eddie Offord was briefly involved and had he remained, the album might have benefited from his production skills, leaving the band to concentrate on the music. Following his exit, Nigel Luby and Geoff Young were responsible for engineering the sessions and in some respects, *Tormato* is Chris Squire's album. Despite the sonic shortcomings, bass guitar is prominent; partly due to the use of effects filters favoured by jazz fusion musicians. Luby was also Squire's friend and personal road manager at the time. Quoted in *Close to the Edge: The Story of Yes* in 1999 Rick had mixed feelings:

Everything was going well and then we did the *Tormato* album in 1978, which was potentially one of the best Yes albums ever. But it suffered from appalling production. By that time, Eddie Offord had gone to Mars and was unavailable. Everybody was using their own engineers, so you never saw so many hands on faders. The whole thing ended up so compressed it was tragic. I would love to get hold of that album and have it remixed. There is some fabulous stuff on there. 'Arriving UFO' is a great track and could have been one of the great Yes stage features of all time, but it suffered on the record.

Seemingly, the radio-friendly sound was in part a conscious attempt to emulate the success of the singles from the previous album. Rick receives more than his usual writing credits, contributing to three songs, while the Anderson / Howe partnership is noticeably less conspicuous than on previous albums. Anderson and Squire co-wrote two of the songs, harking back to *The Yes Album*, and the latter was responsible for the haunting ballad 'Onward'.

Although several songs were performed on the subsequent tour, they did not transfer readily to the stage, and with the occasional exception, were rarely played thereafter. Polymoog and Birotron feature prominently, although they lack the distinctive timbres of the Minimoog and Mellotron. Apart from the tranquil 'Madrigal' and 'Onward' – which both feature real strings rather than Birotron – the songs are awash with Polymoog soloing, Hammond organ is mostly relegated to backing and piano is virtually absent. As a result, the keyboards lack the colour and variety of tone of Rick's previous Yes albums and all too often, Polymoog, guitar and bass seem to be competing rather than working in harmony. Howe was unhappy with the keyboard sounds, feeling that they were incompatible with his guitar parts. He plays a Gibson Les Paul for the most part but reverts to his trusty 175D for the final song.

The doubleheader 'Future Times / Rejoice' gets the album off to a rousing start with Rick's Polymoog fanfare leading the way. It motors along at a brisk pace, driven by Howe's Les Paul flurries and Squire's rasping Rickenbacker, although White's drumming suffers from the soupy mix. Anderson's 'See it all' vocal bridge is a highlight, as is Rick's synth solo at 5:08. The eco-friendly 'Don't Kill the Whale' is a rare protest song from Yes, with Anderson's sparse chorus driving home the message. Released as a single, it peaked at number 36 in the UK chart on 16 September 1978 and the entertaining promo video features the band superimposed over a backdrop of surf and whales. Howe's song 'Abilene' was the B side in the UK. Rick's Polymoog solo at 2:07 is a blast and in the latter part of the song, he produces a suitably wailing tone for the endangered mammals.

Rick was the principal architect of 'Madrigal' with Anderson crooning delightfully over rippling harpsichord and Spanish guitar. Squire and White keep a low profile, providing wordless vocal backing, bass pedals and cymbals. It also boasted a promo video with Rick suitably dressed in period costume. It's a brief respite before the pedal to the metal 'Release, Release' with Anderson's energetic singing underpinned by rhythmic organ chords. The lyrics combine two subjects: the power of rock music and 'the craziness of power' in a political context. Squire's vocal is the most prominent in the bridge and at 2:47, it mimics a live performance complete with drum solo and cheering crowd. Ironically, because of the breathless pace, it proved to be a challenge to perform live. At 4:30, Rick squeezes in another vibrant Polymoog solo before a frantic dash to the finish line and the end of side one.

'Arriving UFO' was inspired by *Close Encounters of the Third Kind,* which had taken cinemas by storm the previous November. It features White's drum synth, which, combined with keyboards, provides some suitably spacey effects while Howe's chattering wah-wah mimics alien voices. The 4/4 synth-propelled instrumental sequence beginning at 3:38 is exhilarating before a simulated explosion and Howe's reverberating Les Paul signals the arrival of the mothership à la *Close Encounters.*

'Circus of Heaven' is either a charming diversion or sentimental indulgence depending upon your tastes. The circus is in town and although Anderson senior is impressed by the spectacle, junior – voiced by Jon's son Damion – isn't. The gleeful verses contrast with a melancholic bridge underscored by Birotron strings before synth leads a merry dance for the finale.

When Squire presented 'Onward' to the band as a basic vocal and piano demo, he knew exactly how he wanted the finished track to sound. It's a beautiful song with an orchestral arrangement of strings and brass courtesy of Squire's old friend Andrew Pryce Jackman from the pre-Yes band The Syn. Rick's Polymoog provides the bass pulse that underpins the song. The instrumental version on the 2004 reissue of *Tormato* is sublime and there's a superb live version on the 1996 *Keys to Ascension* album with Howe's rippling acoustic guitar replicating the pizzicato strings.

The concluding 'On the Silent Wings of Freedom' has the makings of a classic Yes song but fails to deliver on its initial promise. It bursts into life with a monumental bass solo supported by vibrant drumming, Birotron strings and cascading guitar lines. At 2:20, it changes direction with the introduction of the main theme and although Anderson's vocals are assured, the choral hook is not one of Yes' most memorable. An ambient interlude at 4:38 features Birotron and a tolling bell before a sudden burst of energy and fiery synth soloing although the abrupt ending leaves one wanting more. Anderson had not lost his appetite for impressionistic wordplay with 'On the back of your forty-second screamdown' being a prime example.

One of the discarded songs from the sessions, 'Money' recorded on 31 March, surfaced in 1991 on the *Yesyears* box set. The version on the 2004 reissue of *Tormato* features Anderson's singing overdubbed by Rick's humorous commentary.

Hipgnosis was once again responsible for the album artwork and Rick and Steve Howe were especially critical. It's a strong contender for the band's least appealing cover of all time. The album was originally to be titled *Yes Tor*, named after one of the many rocky peaks on Dartmoor, Devon, in the southwest of England. Unfortunately, it isn't particularly photogenic, so the headless image of a man holding divining sticks was added. When this proved to be unsatisfactory, the designer – possibly Aubrey Powell – threw a tomato at it, which, along with the new title, stuck. On the back of the non-gatefold sleeve, the band adopt a Bee Gees style cool, wearing sunglasses and matching bomber jackets.

Understandably, given the potentially hostile musical environment of the late 1970s, *Tormato* received a mixed reception. Like those for Rick's *Criminal Record*, reviews were coloured by the critic's perception of the band and the style of music they embodied. A review in *Creem* magazine in January 1979 by Michael Davis included light-hearted observations on Yes' use of technology:

> Every time Steve Howe finds a rock 'n' roll riff in his Les Paul, he makes it gargle milk and honey and then tickles it to death. Rick Wakeman's found a Birotron (a beer-guzzling Mellotron, didn't ya know) to keep him company. Chris Squire's discovered a bigger bass sound through harmonizers, and Alan White's gone the opposite route with his finely tuned buddies, the Crotales.

Sales of *Tormato* were more than respectable; in America, it was one of Yes' bestselling albums and achieved Platinum status for sales exceeding one million. It entered the UK chart at number 9 and spent 11 weeks in the top 70, reaching a high of 8 during its second week on 14 October

1978. Elsewhere, it made the top 30 in many regions, including Canada, Australia, and most European countries.

Despite some critics ringing the death knell for progressive rock in 1978, genre acts were still holding their own sales-wise including *...And Then There Were Three...* by Genesis, *Hemispheres* by Rush, *Incantations* by Mike Oldfield, *Jeff Wayne's Musical Version of The War of the Worlds*, *Heavy Horses* by Jethro Tull, *Pyramid* by The Alan Parsons Project, *Pieces of Eight* by Styx, *Don't Look Back* by Boston, the eponymous *U.K.* featuring Bill Bruford and debut solo albums from Pink Floyd's David Gilmour and Richard Wright. Tellingly, however, several marked a transition to a more radio-friendly AOR style that would flourish in the 1980s. Released the following year, Supertramp's *Breakfast in America* and Pink Floyd's *The Wall* were two of the bestselling albums of the 1970s.

Tourmato

Yes celebrated their tenth anniversary with a mammoth tour of the USA. It kicked off in Rochester, New York, on 28 August and included four successive dates at New York's Madison Square Garden from 6 to 9 September. The tour was unique; they performed in the round on a circular stage in the middle of the auditorium, allowing more fans to get a closer view of the band. The stage was another innovation from lighting engineer Mike Tait and revolved slowly on rails with Anderson on a central riser and his microphone suspended from the lighting rig. Several songs from *Tormato* were played, including 'Future Times / Rejoice' and 'Release, Release', although the latter was dropped from the setlist in early September. Generally, the new material sounded better live than on the album.

Yes returned to the UK and in the last week of October, they played another string of dates at London's Wembley Arena – formerly the Empire Pool. Wembley is recognised as the home of British sports, especially football, and in the late 1970s, it was also Yes' playground. It was their last shows of 1978 and their only UK appearances that year and such was the demand for tickets, matinee shows were added. A performance on 28 October was recorded by the BBC for *The Friday Rock Show* on Radio One, introduced by Tommy Vance. It remains one of Yes' best recorded and bootlegged concerts of the 1970s, including the *Definitive Tourmato* two CD and DVD. The setlist is classic Yes, although the 'Firebird Suite' introduction is replaced by John William's suspenseful opening cue from *Close Encounters of the Third Kind*. The crashing chord climax is taken up by the band, segueing into the familiar opening riff to 'Siberian Khatru'. *Tormato* is represented by 'Circus of Heaven', 'Don't Kill the Whale' and 'On the Silent Wings of Freedom' with 'Awaken' remaining from the previous album. Otherwise, the set is dominated by songs from *The Yes Album* and *Fragile,* with 'I've Seen All Good People' and 'Roundabout' providing the encores.

Seemingly impervious to the threat of punk, new wave, and disco, Yes' popularity remained undiminished in 1978. In the *Melody Maker* poll winner's awards ceremony in November, all the band members – apart from Alan White – topped their respective categories. Despite the unprecedented popularity of progressive rock and a plethora of classic albums, few books dedicated to the artists were published in the 1970s. *Rick Wakeman: The Caped Crusader* by Dan Wooding was a welcome exception and one of the first prog-related biographies published in the UK. Wooding wrote Rick's first press release in the early 1970s and he was also namechecked in the *Fragile* LP booklet.

Rick was further honoured in 1978 with the excellent tribute album *The Royal Philharmonic Orchestra Performs The Best Known Works Of Rick Wakeman,* released by A&M Records. Arranged and conducted by Richard Hartley, it includes orchestral suites of *King Arthur* and *Journey* plus 'Catherine Howard', 'Anne Boleyn' and 'After the Ball'. The LP cover features colourful illustrations representing Rick's albums surrounding a photo of the RPO on stage. The orchestra was, however, recorded in the studio by producers Hartley and Robin Geoffrey Cable, who utilised a ground-breaking technique. Instead of recording the combined orchestra as was standard practice, they were recorded in sections with each instrument individually miked. The result is a sonic clarity that outshines the original recordings. The lengthy sleeve notes include:

[Artists conversant with both classical and popular music include] Rick Wakeman who was one of a new style of rock musician to emerge in the late 1960s. These were serious composers and virtuoso performers, many of whom were classically trained, attracted by the possibilities of experimenting in the more sophisticated forms of rock created by the development of a market for albums of contemporary music. With them, they brought a new level of expertise and a distinctive approach that was to dominate the next decade.

1979 - All Things Must Pass

I can't do this anymore. It's time for me to leave.
Jon Anderson quoted by Rick in the *Say Yes!* autobiography.

The final year of the 1970s proved to be one of the most tumultuous in Rick's career and the history of Yes. After a gap of five months, the *Tormato* tour resumed in Kalamazoo, Michigan on 9 April. It was the start of an arduous three-month North American trek that included cities they had bypassed on the previous outing. A show highlight captured on the Yes *Live in Philadelphia 1979* video recorded on 21 June features Rick wielding a hefty keytar, sparring with Howe and Squire during the climax of 'Starship Trooper'. When the tour concluded at the Hollywood Sportatorium in Florida on 30 June, it would be more than a year before Yes returned to the stage, and more significantly, it was Rick's final appearance with the band for more than a decade. In the interim, he had a new album in the pipeline, which would be his last for A&M Records.

Rick Wakeman - Rhapsodies

Personnel:
Rick Wakeman: keyboards, vocoder vocals on 'Pedra da Gávea'
Nico Ramsden: electric guitar
Tony Visconti: acoustic guitar, engineer
Bruce Lynch: bass guitars
Frank Gibson Jr: drums and percussion
Produced at La Grange Studios using Mobile One and Mountain Studios, Montreux, Switzerland by Tony Visconti
Recording date: 1978 – 1979
Release date: May 1979
Record label: A&M
Highest chart places: UK: 25, USA: 170
Running time: 70:25
All tracks written by Rick Wakeman, except as noted otherwise
Side one: 1. Pedra De Gavea (4:11), 2. Front Line (3:42), 3. Bombay Duck (3:14), 4. Animal Showdown (Yes We Have No Bananas) (2:40) (Rick Wakeman, Frank Silver, Irving Cohn), 5. Big Ben (3:58). Side two: 1. Rhapsody in Blue (5:26) (George Gershwin), 2. Woolly Willy Tango (3:24), 3. The Pulse (5:21), 4. Swan Lager (Pyotr Tchaikovsky, Edvard Grieg) (2:50). Side three:

1. March of the Gladiators (4:53), 2. Flacons De Neige (5:01), 3. The Flasher (5:32), 4. The Palais (2:23). Side four: 1. Stand-By (3:30), 2. Sea Horses (3:52), 3. Half Holiday (3:00), 4. Summertime (4:27) (Gershwin), 5. Credits (3:10)

With Rick's album sales diminishing at a progressive rate, his final release of the 1970s had one eye on the singles market. Despite it being a double LP, there is no concept or extravagant trimmings and the 18 tracks average around the radio-friendly, four-minute mark. In *Classic Rock* magazine in 2012, Rick described *Rhapsodies* as: 'The end of an era in many ways'.

He was still a tax exile in Switzerland, and it was the second of three solo albums he recorded at Mountain Studios, Montreux. At this juncture, A&M Records were calling the shots and brought in a producer to steer Rick in a more commercial direction. Fortunately, he and Rick went back a long way, having worked together on the Strawbs albums and numerous session recordings. Rick reflected in *Classic Rock*:

The album is probably the most confusing I've made. It contains so many differing styles that it's hard to keep track of what the album is all about. A&M decided I had to have a producer and Tony Visconti was brought on board, who I got on great with. A&M demanded disco – please! I know, and that's how 'Rhapsody in Blue' came about – plus all sorts of other styles, some of which I loved and some of which I didn't. Great sounds on tracks like 'March of the Gladiators', though.

After the essential *Criminal Record* eighteen months earlier, several tracks seem like filler and thanks to Visconti's commercial gleam, it's Rick's most dated-sounding album of the 1970s. The disco beats are firmly rooted in the 1970s and, by 1979, were already sounding passé. In addition to Mountain Studios – which was bought out by Queen that same year – a mobile unit was utilised for the recording, although it proved to be a difficult task manoeuvring it along the twisting mountain roads. Visconti hired session musicians Bruce Lynch and Frank Gibson Jr, a finely tuned rhythm partnership, and the versatile Nico Ramsden, who played on Mike Oldfield's *Exposed* and *Platinum* albums, also released in 1979.

Speaking of Mike Oldfield, there's several interesting parallels that link his work with Rick's in the 1970s. They both released their mostly instrumental debut albums in 1973 and were jointly responsible for pioneering long-form music with classical influences in a traditional rock setting. Their final albums of the 1970s – *Rhapsodies* and *Platinum* – are also arguably their weakest of the decade, failing to live up to the opulent titles. Finally, both albums include a George Gershwin cover.

The opening track, 'Pedra da Gavea', takes its name from the mountain near Rio de Janeiro and the melody is a leftover from the *No Earthly Connection* sessions. The only track to feature Rick's vocoder-treated vocals, it's built around a rasping bass line and the Bo Diddley shuffle beat. For much of side one, Visconti's bright production has plenty of light, but little in the way of shade and the tracks maintain a persistent upbeat tempo. Rick has not lost his touch, however, and his speed and dexterity during 'Front Line' are breathtaking and the backing trio certainly know their chops. The musical clichés of 'Bombay Duck' are more Middle Eastern than Indian, while the equally jaunty 'Animal Showdown' features nimble Minimoog playing. During 'Big Ben', Rick lets fly with some equally impressive synth fireworks.

On side two, Rick remains faithful to Gershwin's masterpiece 'Rhapsody in Blue' with a dazzling display of orchestral synths and piano. Visconti is responsible for the arrangement and only the disco rhythm that kicks in after 20 seconds lets the side down. 'Woolly Willy Tango' is perhaps best remembered for the entertaining promo video featuring sensual dance routines and footage of Rick in performance. 'The Pulse' features another persistent disco beat while 'Swan Lager' opts for a cod reggae rhythm for a breezy rendition of 'Swan Lake'. At 1:13, it morphs into Grieg's 'Piano Concerto in A Minor' before returning to Tchaikovsky's ballet theme.

Side three is possibly the album's most successful and opens in style with 'March of the Gladiators'. It's not to be confused with the 1897 march 'Entry of the Gladiators' – better known as the 'Circus Song' – by Czech composer Julius Fučík. It has a similar pomp and grandeur with soaring synths, chunky organ chords, a compelling melody and blistering Moog soloing. The sublime theme that opens and closes 'Flacons De Neige' wouldn't have been out of place on *The Six Wives* album, although the keyboard timbres date it somewhat. Despite the tongue-in-cheek title, the edgy 'The Flasher' is one of the album's proggiest offerings, while 'The Palais' is a haunting piano solo that could only come from the fingers of Rick Wakeman.

Side four hits the ground running with the staccato chords and exuberant melody of 'Stand-By', another album highlight. The ambient

'Sea Horses' with its moody fretless bass is a piece that Rick would return to in later years, both on stage and *The Classical Connection* album in 1991. 'Half Holiday' is sure to put a smile on anyone's face, with Rick doing a remarkable job of replicating the sound of a trad jazz band in full swing. On the penultimate track, his masterful piano interpretation of Gershwin's 'Summertime' would be replicated on the *Piano Portraits* album in 2017.

The LP release of *Rhapsodies* in some regions excludes the final track 'Credits' although it's present and correct on the UK version. True to the title, Rick's spoken commentary acknowledges the contributions of Ramsden, Gibson, Lynch, Visconti, and himself – 'It's my bloody album after all' – over a mock, cheering audience and comical musical backing. It's not the most inspired ending to a Rick Wakeman album, but some 33 years later, Henry Yates' retrospective review in *Classic Rock* accented the positives:

Rhapsodies is all over the shop, but pan through these tracks and you'll find gold. Despite the intimidating four sides of vinyl, it generally feels less dense and cerebral than Wakeman's past progging, with the electro-flavoured track-listing reading like his order at the local takeaway – 'Bombay Duck', 'Swan Lager' – and moments like the daft squelch of 'Woolly Willy Tango' prompting genuine affection.

Rick's groomed appearance on the gatefold sleeve is in keeping with the modulated tone of the album. In the background, the Matterhorn and a family with their pet dog are strangely wrapped in baking foil and on the centre spread, a flying Rick is 'playing' the keys with his hands and feet. The snow-covered mountains on the cover possibly struck a chord in Norway, where *Rhapsodies* charted at number 15. On 16 June, it peaked at 25 in the UK, the same position as *Criminal Record,* although at ten weeks, *Rhapsodies* spent twice as long in the top 100. *Rhapsodies* struggled in most other regions, including America where it stalled in the lower region of the Billboard top 200. It's Rick's only album of the 1970s without a linking theme, and in the June 1987 edition of *Home Keyboard Review* magazine, he said:

I started with *Henry VIII,* then moved onto *Journey* and *Arthur.* Then people suggested that I tried different things, so I tried them, and they were reasonably successful but not as successful as the concepts. I keep getting told by people and the record company that the concept thing [has] finished and I keep saying to myself, 'no it hasn't'.

Looking back at the bestselling rock albums of the 1970s in the UK and USA, familiar names like Led Zeppelin, Pink Floyd, the Eagles, Boston, Foreigner, Queen, Fleetwood Mac, and the Rolling Stones figure prominently. Although Rick's success was modest in comparison, he can be justly proud of his legacy in a decade where rock music and the songwriters and musicians truly came of age. With their virtuoso technique, mastery of keyboard technology and music that was both ambitious and popular, Rick and Keith Emerson were recognised as the foremost rock keyboardists of their generation. Their styles, however, were very different. Emerson's piano playing was informed by jazz pioneers Oscar Peterson and Dave Brubeck and his penchant for 20th-century classical composers like Aaron Copland and Alberto Ginastera is evident throughout his work. Rick's playing is flamboyant but less showy and he's less inclined to quote classical pieces in his music. In 1977, Rick identified his favourite classical composers as Mozart for his melodies and Rachmaninoff for his orchestration. They both influenced his piano playing and he's remained a lifelong fan of Prokofiev for his early inspiration.

The End of an Era
In the summer of 1979, at his home studio in Surrey, Chris Squire, along with *Tormato* sound engineers Nigel Luby and Geoff Young, sifted through several years of tour tapes for the proposed *Yesshows* live album. It was to be the long-awaited follow-up to *Yessongs* from six years earlier with new artwork by Roger Dean, his first for Yes since *Yesterdays* in 1975. When the band couldn't agree on a final mix, the release was put on hold until after the next studio album.

On 19 July, Rick and his band played a selection of music from *The Six Wives, Journey, King Arthur, No Earthly Connection* and *Rhapsodies* at the annual Montreux Jazz Festival. When Rick was joined by Jon Anderson for the second part of the set, they performed a piano and harp duet, 'Leaves of Green', 'Flight of the Moorglade', and two extended jams, accompanied by Steve Howe for the latter. The same day, Howe performed a solo set. In August, Rick played three continuous nights at the recently opened The Venue music club in Victoria Street, London.

Rick was still based in Montreux and *Rock n' Roll Prophet* was the last of the trio of albums he recorded at Mountain Studios. Due to contractual complications, it wasn't released until 1982 on Rick's Moon Records label, launched earlier that year. Recorded on a tight budget, it's mostly a solo effort with Rick's treated vocals gracing three tracks. The novelty opening song 'I'm So Straight I'm a Weirdo' was released as a UK single in 1980, but despite an entertaining promo video starring Rick as a city gent, it failed to chart. It was his final release for A&M Records, the label he had been with for precisely ten years.

It would be an understatement to say that *Rock n' Roll Prophet* is not Rick's finest hour – or rather 36 minutes – which was the original playing time before the extended reissue in 1991. Clearly, Rick was attempting to emulate the synth-pop popular at the time, but tonally, the album lacks depth and colour. 'The Dragon' and the title track that closes the album are built around repetitive synth motifs and a basic rhythm track, although the latter does end with a grand flourish. Both 'Dark' and 'Early Warning' attempt to convey a sense of stately grandeur and would have benefited from more adventurous arrangements. 'Maybe '80' sounds like it had one eye on the singles market with Rick's vocal backed by a jaunty Polymoog melody and the instrumental 'Spy of 55' is in a similar novelty pop vein. The whimsical 'Do You Believe in Fairies?' was also the B side of the 'I'm So Straight I'm a Weirdo' single and, with its gimmicky vocals and tone, owes an obvious debt to David Bowie's 'The Laughing Gnome'.

Rick wasn't the only one keeping himself busy with non-Yes activities. *The Steve Howe Album* was the guitarist's second solo outing and Jon Anderson collaborated with Vangelis for their debut album *Short Stories*.

In November, Yes reconvened en masse in Paris to rehearse and record the successor to *Tormato*. The French capital was a compromise being roughly halfway between London and Montreux, although none of the band members particularly wanted to be there, especially Howe and Squire, who preferred to record in London. Moreover, there was no clear agreement on which direction the music should take and a rift within the band grew as work progressed.

Howe, Squire and White jammed for several days as a power trio centred on guitar, bass, and drums, taking the music in a heavier direction. This was counter to the style Anderson and Rick had in mind and the material they presented when they joined the sessions did not go down too well with the other three. Speaking to *Prog* magazine in 2014, Rick confirmed:

In Paris, not only were we not on the same road, but we were not even heading in the same direction! Jon and I had put some songs together during the previous tour and we felt they had great potential. Sadly, this was not felt by Steve, Chris and Alan, and sessions in the studio were laborious and not pleasant at all.

Brian Lane brought Queen producer Roy Thomas Baker in to act as a mediator, but he found the band at this stage impossible to work with and left after a few weeks. The situation was resolved when Alan White went roller skating with Virgin Records founder and entrepreneur Richard Branson and broke his ankle, bringing the sessions to an end. The unreleased tracks recorded in Paris would later surface on bootlegs, box sets and as bonus tracks on album reissues. Some of the material was also reworked for solo albums.

The recordings are generally more harmonious than the rift suggests, especially when all the band are contributing. Rick provides a symphonic backdrop to mellow songs like Anderson's 'Picasso' and Squire's 'You Can Be Saved' while those co-written by Jon and Rick are generally upbeat, mid-tempo offerings. 'Never Done Before' features electric piano and a sprightly honky tonk piano break, while 'Tango' is so named because of the 4/4 keyboard rhythm, which Rick embellishes with synth fills. Both songs appear on the *In a Word: Yes (1969–)* box set released in 2002. 'In a Tower', which benefits from a backdrop of rich Hammond organ chords, was a bonus track on the 2004 CD reissue of *Drama*. Closing the same album, 'Friend of a Friend' motors along at a brisk pace, although the Polymoog flourishes are almost buried beneath the weight of bass and drums. Also, on the *Drama* reissue, the triumphant synth theme in 'Golden Age' is a variation of 'Maybe '80' on the *Rock n' Roll Prophet* album.

Following the Paris sessions, Yes returned to England for the Christmas holidays and agreed to reconvene early in the new year. Jon and Rick suggested the band take several months out to recharge their batteries, but the others were keen to forge ahead with the album. Anderson headed for Barbados to write new lyrics while Howe, Squire, and White continued rehearsals at Redan Recorders in London. Howe confirmed the arrangement to biographer Dan Hedges:

He (Rick) was going to rehearse with us for a week, go back to Switzerland, we were going to record the backing tracks, and he was going to come back and record his parts later.

Rick didn't come back. In *Yes: The Authorised Biography*, he said:

I think everybody knew that the line-up, as it was, had between three and five years to run. I had hoped it would run for the five years. It became obvious in 1979 that it couldn't.

He had also exhausted the quota of days a tax exile was allowed in the UK. When Anderson returned from Barbados and presented his lyrics, they didn't sit comfortably with the cutting-edge sound conceived in his absence. He also questioned the band's finances, resulting in a heated argument and Anderson's departure. For Rick, it was the final straw; he could not envisage a Yes without their founding lead singer. His and Anderson's exit from the band was officially announced in March 1980. It was an unceremonious close to an eventful decade. In the *Yes Music Circle* magazine in February 1993, bassist Roger Newell had this to say about Rick's work ethic in the 1970s:

Like many great artists, he suffers for it. Whether he still does or not, I've no idea, but I bet he probably does. He used to give his all, there was nothing left. You can't ask more than that of anybody. We were much more confident and felt easier than him because our livelihood wasn't on the line if it went wrong. We wouldn't have got blamed – he would have done.

Epilogue

Although Rick's popularity faltered in the 1980s, he continued doing what he did best, recording new music and performing live. As of the time of writing, January 2023, Rick continues to tour with a reformed English Rock Ensemble, although the line-up has changed significantly from the 1970s. His prolific output from 1981 onwards embraces rock, prog, new age, film soundtracks, solo piano, classical, Christian faith, and live recordings. When interviewed by Bob Harris for BBC Radio One on 9 February 1993, Rick was candid about his output in the post-1970s era:

> There were a lot of reasons [for] getting involved in different types of music. One was called 'paying the mortgage' because the 80s was tough, Bob, I'll tell you. And it's still tough out there now. The music industry is not easy for anybody. I wanted to continue to make music and make records and I couldn't always make what I wanted to do. So, you look around for an area where you can perform and you can play within the budget, however limited it is, that you've got.

Rick's sense of humour hasn't diminished, and in *Classic Rock* magazine in 2012, he quipped that in 1980, he couldn't even get a job as a piano tuner. As a vehicle for his recordings, Rick launched his own record labels, including Moon in 1982, Ambient in 1990 and Hope in 1995, which all eventually folded due to high running costs. Rick was also eager to get into broadcasting and in 1982, he co-hosted the UK Channel 4 TV series *Gastank* with fellow keyboardist Tony Ashton. In 1987, Rick released one of his most treasured works *The Gospels,* which he would revisit both live and on album in subsequent years.

Rick continued his on-and-off relationship with Yes, including the band's offshoots, Anderson Bruford Wakeman Howe in 1988 and Anderson, Rabin and Wakeman in 2016. He reunited with the classic Yes line-up in 1990, 1995 and 2002 but spent just two years with the band on each occasion. Band politics, disagreements and managerial interference were the usual causes, but Rick has remained a Yes fan even when he's been absent from the band. He was vocal in his condemnation of the 1991 *Union* album but enjoyed the subsequent tour, where he developed a friendship with Trevor Rabin. He was scheduled to contribute to a 1993 Yes album, which failed to materialise due to the 6,000 miles that separated Rick from the rest of the band based on the American west coast.

A consummate showman, Rick took to the stage in a variety of guises in the 1990s. Your author caught one of the *Wakeman with Wakeman* rock shows in 1992, a performance of *The Gospels* at Bradford Cathedral in October 1993, and *An Evening with Rick Wakeman* solo routine combining keyboards with stand-up comedy at Leeds City Varieties Music Hall in February 2000. His album output in the 1990s was prolific and *Return to the Centre of the Earth* released at the end of the decade, saw a rare return to the charts. A steady stream of live recordings included several from the 1970s, providing a welcome opportunity to witness Rick in his prime. On *The Legend: Live In Concert 2000* DVD, Rick's reference to Jon Anderson remains the singer's favourite quote about himself: 'He's the only person I know who's trying to save the planet by living on a totally different one'.

In the new millennium, Rick toured extensively with the English Rock Ensemble, solo, with Yes and as one half of Anderson/Wakeman. His profile as a TV personality and raconteur was raised with the popular BBC series *Grumpy Old Men* and he also hosted his own show on *Planet Rock* radio. As a tribute to David Bowie, who died in January 2016, Rick recorded a solo piano version of 'Life on Mars?' and the same year, his sartorial dress sense was celebrated by The Fleshtones with the satirical song 'Rick Wakeman's Cape'. The *Piano Portraits* album in January 2017 marked Rick's return to the UK top 10 and later that year, as a former member of Yes, he was inducted into the Rock and Roll Hall of Fame.

In 2020, *The Red Planet* album heralded a return to prog rock form for the 71-year-old Rick and in 2022, *The Myths and Legends of Rick Wakeman* box set gathered four live performances from the mid-1970s. In 2021, he was appointed Commander of the Order of the British Empire (CBE) for services to music and broadcasting and he is also active in animal rights.

Rick's itinerary with the ERE continues, including in 2023 two shows at the London Palladium billed as *The Return of The Caped Crusader*, featuring music from *The Six Wives, Journey, King Arthur* and Yes. This was very fitting, given that 2023 is the 50th Anniversary of Rick's debut solo album. There were also solo dates, including solo shows in the USA under the heading *Rick Wakeman – His Music & Stories*. Both Strawbs and Yes continue to release albums and tour, although without their former keyboardist. I will let Rick's son Adam have the final word with this salient observation in *Classic Rock* in 2012:

I know that one of the things that frustrates my dad as an artist and a musician is that people play things too safe nowadays and they have done for such a long time. It's a complete role reversal of how things were done in the 70s, with people now touring just to maintain an income, so they can make records that don't make money. Which is, unfortunately, the way things are. It's just evolution.

Bibliography

Books

Wooding, D., *Rick Wakeman: The Caped Crusader* (Robert Hale, 1978)
Hedges, D., *Yes: The Authorised Biography* (Sidgwick & Jackson, 1981)
Wakeman, R., *Say Yes!* (Hodder & Stoughton, 1995)
Welch, C., *Close to the Edge: The Story of Yes* (Omnibus Press, 1999)
Watkinson, D., *Yes: Perpetual Change* (Plexus, 2001)
Emerson, K., *Pictures of an Exhibitionist* (John Blake, 2004)
Farley, A., *The Extraordinary World of Yes* (iUniverse, 2004)
Visconti, T., *Bowie, Bolan and the Brooklyn Boy* (HarperCollins, 2007)
Bruford, B., *Bill Bruford: The Autobiography* (Jawbone, 2009)
Cousins, D., *Exorcising Ghosts: Strawbs & Other Lives* (Witchwood Media, 2014)
Popoff, M., *Time and a Word: The Yes Story* (Soundcheck Books, 2016)
Romano, W., *Close to the Edge: How Yes' Masterpiece Defined Prog Rock* (Backbeat Books, 2017)
Jones, D., *David Bowie: A Life* (Preface Publishing, 2017)

Magazine Resources

Melody Maker
New Musical Express
Sounds
Disc
Yes Music Circle
Classic Rock
Prog
Billboard
Rolling Stone
Creem
The Guitar Magazine
Home Keyboard Review

Newspapers

The Sunday Times
The Guardian
The Observer
Daily Mirror
Daily Telegraph

Sleeve Notes
The Royal Philharmonic Orchestra Performs The Best Known Works Of Rick Wakeman – A&M Records (1978)

Tour Programme Notes
An Evening with Rick Wakeman – UK (2000)
Yes *Full Circle Tour* – UK (2003)

Videos
Yesyears documentary (Warner VHS, 1991)
Yes *Classic Artists* documentary (Black Hill DVD, 2008)

Online resources
www.rwcc.com – Rick Wakeman's official website
www.nfte.org – Yes source website
www.thestar.com – Toronto Star news website
www.theguardian.com – The Guardian news website

On Track series
Alan Parsons Project – Steve Swift 978-1-78952-154-2
Tori Amos – Lisa Torem 978-1-78952-142-9
Asia – Peter Braidis 978-1-78952-099-6
Badfinger – Robert Day-Webb 978-1-878952-176-4
Barclay James Harvest – Keith and Monica Domone 978-1-78952-067-5
The Beatles – Andrew Wild 978-1-78952-009-5
The Beatles Solo 1969-1980 – Andrew Wild 978-1-78952-030-9
Blue Oyster Cult – Jacob Holm-Lupo 978-1-78952-007-1
Blur – Matt Bishop – 978-178952-164-1
Marc Bolan and T.Rex – Peter Gallagher 978-1-78952-124-5
Kate Bush – Bill Thomas 978-1-78952-097-2
Camel – Hamish Kuzminski 978-1-78952-040-8
Caravan – Andy Boot 978-1-78952-127-6
Cardiacs – Eric Benac 978-1-78952-131-3
Eric Clapton Solo – Andrew Wild 978-1-78952-141-2
The Clash – Nick Assirati 978-1-78952-077-4
Crosby, Stills and Nash – Andrew Wild 978-1-78952-039-2
The Damned – Morgan Brown 978-1-78952-136-8
Deep Purple and Rainbow 1968-79 – Steve Pilkington 978-1-78952-002-6
Dire Straits – Andrew Wild 978-1-78952-044-6
The Doors – Tony Thompson 978-1-78952-137-5
Dream Theater – Jordan Blum 978-1-78952-050-7
Electric Light Orchestra – Barry Delve 978-1-78952-152-8
Elvis Costello and The Attractions – Georg Purvis 978-1-78952-129-0
Emerson Lake and Palmer – Mike Goode 978-1-78952-000-2
Fairport Convention – Kevan Furbank 978-1-78952-051-4
Peter Gabriel – Graeme Scarfe 978-1-78952-138-2
Genesis – Stuart MacFarlane 978-1-78952-005-7
Gentle Giant – Gary Steel 978-1-78952-058-3
Gong – Kevan Furbank 978-1-78952-082-8
Hall and Oates – Ian Abrahams 978-1-78952-167-2
Hawkwind – Duncan Harris 978-1-78952-052-1
Peter Hammill – Richard Rees Jones 978-1-78952-163-4
Roy Harper – Opher Goodwin 978-1-78952-130-6
Jimi Hendrix – Emma Stott 978-1-78952-175-7
The Hollies – Andrew Darlington 978-1-78952-159-7
Iron Maiden – Steve Pilkington 978-1-78952-061-3
Jefferson Airplane – Richard Butterworth 978-1-78952-143-6
Jethro Tull – Jordan Blum 978-1-78952-016-3
Elton John in the 1970s – Peter Kearns 978-1-78952-034-7
The Incredible String Band – Tim Moon 978-1-78952-107-8
Iron Maiden – Steve Pilkington 978-1-78952-061-3
Judas Priest – John Tucker 978-1-78952-018-7
Kansas – Kevin Cummings 978-1-78952-057-6
The Kinks – Martin Hutchinson 978-1-78952-172-6
Korn – Matt Karpe 978-1-78952-153-5
Led Zeppelin – Steve Pilkington 978-1-78952-151-1
Level 42 – Matt Philips 978-1-78952-102-3

Little Feat – 978-1-78952-168-9
Aimee Mann – Jez Rowden 978-1-78952-036-1
Joni Mitchell – Peter Kearns 978-1-78952-081-1
The Moody Blues – Geoffrey Feakes 978-1-78952-042-2
Motorhead – Duncan Harris 978-1-78952-173-3
Mike Oldfield – Ryan Yard 978-1-78952-060-6
Opeth – Jordan Blum 978-1-78-952-166-5
Tom Petty – Richard James 978-1-78952-128-3
Porcupine Tree – Nick Holmes 978-1-78952-144-3
Queen – Andrew Wild 978-1-78952-003-3
Radiohead – William Allen 978-1-78952-149-8
Renaissance – David Detmer 978-1-78952-062-0
The Rolling Stones 1963-80 – Steve Pilkington 978-1-78952-017-0
The Smiths and Morrissey – Tommy Gunnarsson 978-1-78952-140-5
Status Quo the Frantic Four Years – Richard James 978-1-78952-160-3
Steely Dan – Jez Rowden 978-1-78952-043-9
Steve Hackett – Geoffrey Feakes 978-1-78952-098-9
Thin Lizzy – Graeme Stroud 978-1-78952-064-4
Toto – Jacob Holm-Lupo 978-1-78952-019-4
U2 – Eoghan Lyng 978-1-78952-078-1
UFO – Richard James 978-1-78952-073-6
The Who – Geoffrey Feakes 978-1-78952-076-7
Roy Wood and the Move – James R Turner 978-1-78952-008-8
Van Der Graaf Generator – Dan Coffey 978-1-78952-031-6
Yes – Stephen Lambe 978-1-78952-001-9
Frank Zappa 1966 to 1979 – Eric Benac 978-1-78952-033-0
Warren Zevon – Peter Gallagher 978-1-78952-170-2
10CC – Peter Kearns 978-1-78952-054-5

Decades Series
The Bee Gees in the 1960s – Andrew Môn Hughes et al 978-1-78952-148-1
The Bee Gees in the 1970s – Andrew Môn Hughes et al 978-1-78952-179-5
Black Sabbath in the 1970s – Chris Sutton 978-1-78952-171-9
Britpop – Peter Richard Adams and Matt Pooler 978-1-78952-169-6
Alice Cooper in the 1970s – Chris Sutton 978-1-78952-104-7
Curved Air in the 1970s – Laura Shenton 978-1-78952-069-9
Bob Dylan in the 1980s – Don Klees 978-1-78952-157-3
Fleetwood Mac in the 1970s – Andrew Wild 978-1-78952-105-4
Focus in the 1970s – Stephen Lambe 978-1-78952-079-8
Free and Bad Company in the 1970s – John Van der Kiste 978-1-78952-178-8
Genesis in the 1970s – Bill Thomas 978178952-146-7
George Harrison in the 1970s – Eoghan Lyng 978-1-78952-174-0
Marillion in the 1980s – Nathaniel Webb 978-1-78952-065-1
Mott the Hoople and Ian Hunter in the 1970s – John Van der Kiste
978-1-78-952-162-7
Pink Floyd In The 1970s – Georg Purvis 978-1-78952-072-9
Tangerine Dream in the 1970s – Stephen Palmer 978-1-78952-161-0
The Sweet in the 1970s – Darren Johnson from Gary Cosby collection
978-1-78952-139-9
Uriah Heep in the 1970s – Steve Pilkington 978-1-78952-103-0

Yes in the 1980s – Stephen Lambe with David Watkinson 978-1-78952-125-2

On Screen series
Carry On... – Stephen Lambe 978-1-78952-004-0
David Cronenberg – Patrick Chapman 978-1-78952-071-2
Doctor Who: The David Tennant Years – Jamie Hailstone 978-1-78952-066-8
James Bond – Andrew Wild – 978-1-78952-010-1
Monty Python – Steve Pilkington 978-1-78952-047-7
Seinfeld Seasons 1 to 5 – Stephen Lambe 978-1-78952-012-5

Other Books
1967: A Year In Psychedelic Rock – Kevan Furbank 978-1-78952-155-9
1970: A Year In Rock – John Van der Kiste 978-1-78952-147-4
1973: The Golden Year of Progressive Rock 978-1-78952-165-8
Babysitting A Band On The Rocks – G.D. Praetorius 978-1-78952-106-1
Eric Clapton Sessions – Andrew Wild 978-1-78952-177-1
Derek Taylor: For Your Radioactive Children – Andrew Darlington 978-1-78952-038-5
The Golden Road: The Recording History of The Grateful Dead – John Kilbride 978-1-78952-156-6
Iggy and The Stooges On Stage 1967-1974 – Per Nilsen 978-1-78952-101-6
Jon Anderson and the Warriors – the road to Yes – David Watkinson 978-1-78952-059-0
Nu Metal: A Definitive Guide – Matt Karpe 978-1-78952-063-7
Tommy Bolin: In and Out of Deep Purple – Laura Shenton 978-1-78952-070-5
Maximum Darkness – Deke Leonard 978-1-78952-048-4
Maybe I Should've Stayed In Bed – Deke Leonard 978-1-78952-053-8
The Twang Dynasty – Deke Leonard 978-1-78952-049-1

and many more to come!

Would you like to write for Sonicbond Publishing?

At Sonicbond Publishing, we are always on the lookout for authors, particularly for our two main series. At the moment, we only accept books on music-related subjects.

On Track. Mixing fact with in-depth analysis, the On Track series examines the work of a particular musical artist or group. All genres are considered, from easy listening and jazz to 60s soul to 90s pop, via rock and metal.

Decades. An in-depth look at an important calendar decade in the career of a well-known artist or group.

While professional writing experience would, of course, be an advantage, the most important qualification is to have real enthusiasm and knowledge of your subject. First-time authors are welcomed, but the ability to write well in English is essential.

Sonicbond Publishing has distribution throughout Europe, North America and Australia and all books will also published in E-book form. Authors will be paid a royalty based on sales.

Further details are available from www.sonicbondpublishing.co.uk.

To get in touch, complete the contact form there or email info@sonicbondpublishing.co.uk

Follow us on social media:
Twitter: https://twitter.com/SonicbondP
Instagram: https://www.instagram.com/sonicbondpublishing_/
Facebook: https://www.facebook.com/SonicbondPublishing/

Linktree QR code: